LIFE AT HIGH TIDE

Harper's Novelettes

Edited By

William Dean Howells and Henry Mills Alden

1ST WORLD
LIBRARY
Literary Society

Life at High Tide

Various Authors

© 1st World Library, 2007
PO Box 2211
Fairfield, IA 52556
www.1stworldlibrary.com
First Edition

LCCN: 2007934208

Softcover ISBN: 978-1-4218-9680-9
Hardcover ISBN: 978-1-4218-9780-6
eBook ISBN: 978-1-4218-9580-2

Purchase *"Life at High Tide"*
as a traditional bound book at:
www.1stWorldLibrary.com/purchase.asp?ISBN=978-1-4218-9680-9

1st World Library is a literary, educational organization
dedicated to:

- Creating a free internet library of downloadable ebooks

- Hosting writing competitions and offering book publishing
scholarships.

Interested in more 1st World Library books? contact:
literacy@1stworldlibrary.com
Check us out at: www.1stworldlibrary.com

1ˢᵗ World Library Literary Society

Giving Back to the World

"If you want to work on the core problem, it's early school literacy."

- James Barksdale, former CEO of Netscape

"No skill is more crucial to the future of a child, or to a democratic and prosperous society, than literacy."

- Los Angeles Times

"Literacy... means far more than learning how to read and write... The aim is to transmit... knowledge and promote social participation."

- UNESCO

"Literacy is not a luxury, it is a right and a responsibility. If our world is to meet the challenges of the twenty-first century we must harness the energy and creativity of all our citizens."

- President Bill Clinton

"Parents should be encouraged to read to their children, and teachers should be equipped with all available techniques for teaching literacy, so the varying needs and capacities of individual kids can be taken into account."

- Hugh Mackay

CONTENTS

PREFACE

There is a tide in the affairs of men
Which, taken at the flood, leads on to fortune.

Thus the poet—and poetry, of the old order at least, always waiting upon great events, has found in the high-tide flotations of masterful heroes to fortune themes most flatteringly responsive to its own high tension.

The writer of fiction has no such afflatus, no such high pitch of life, as to outward circumstance, in his representation of it, as the poet has; and therefore his may seem to the academic critic the lesser art—but it is nearer to the realities of common human existence. He deals with plain men and women, and the un-majestic moments of their lives.

"Life at High Tide"—the title selected for this little volume of short stories, and having a real significance for each of them, which the reader may find out for himself—does not reflect the poet's meaning, and, least of all, its easy optimism. In every one of these stories is presented a critical moment in one individual life—sometimes, as in "The Glass Door" and in "Elizabeth and Davie," in two lives; but it leads not to or away from fortune—it simply discloses character; also, in situations like those so vividly depicted in "Keepers of a Charge" and "A Yearly Tribute," the tense strain of modern circumstance. In all these real instances there are luminous points of idealism—of an idealism implicit but translucent.

The authors here represented have won exceptional distinction as short-story writers, and the examples given of their work not only are typical of the best periodical fiction of a very recent period—all of them having been published within five years—but illustrate the distinctive features, as unprecedented in quality as they are diversified in character, which mark the extreme advance in this field of literature.

H. M. A.

THE IMMEDIATE JEWEL

BY MARGARET DELAND

"*Good name, in man and woman, dear my lord,
Is* the immediate jewel of their souls."

—Othello

I

When James Graham, carpenter, enlisted, it was with the assurance that if he lost his life his grateful country would provide for his widow. He did lose it, and Mrs. Graham received, in exchange for a husband and his small earnings, the sum of $12 a month. But when you own your own very little house, with a dooryard for chickens (and such stray dogs and cats as quarter themselves upon you), and enough grass for a cow, and a friendly neighbor to remember your potato-barrel, why, you can get along—somehow. In Lizzie Graham's case nobody knew just how, because she was not one of the confidential kind. But certainly there were days in winter when the house was chilly, and months when fresh meat was unknown, and years when a new dress was not thought of. This state of things is not remarkable, taken in connection with an income of $144 a year, and a New England village where people all do their own work, so that a woman has no chance to hire out.

All the same, Mrs. Graham was not an object of charity. Had she been that, she would have been promptly sent to the Poor Farm. No sentimental consideration of a grateful country would have moved Jonesville to philanthropy; it sent its paupers to the Poor Farm with prompt common sense.

When Jonesville's old school-teacher, Mr. Nathaniel May, came wandering back from the great world, quite penniless, almost blind, and with a faint mist across his pleasant mind, Jonesville saw nothing for him but the Poor Farm.... Nathaniel had been away from home for many years; rumors came back, occasionally, that he was going to make his fortune by some patent, and Jonesville said that if he did it would be a good thing for the town, for Nathaniel wasn't one to forget his friends. "He'll give us a library," said Jonesville, grinning; "Nat was a great un for books." However, Jonesville was still without its library, when, one August day, the stage dropped a gentle, forlorn figure at the door of Dyer's Hotel.

"I'm Nat May," he said; "well, it's good to get home!"

He brought with him, as the sum of his possessions, a dilapidated leather hand-bag full of strange wheels and little reflectors, and small, scratched lenses; the poor clothes upon his back; and twenty-four cents in his pocket. He walked hesitatingly, with one hand outstretched to feel his way, for he was nearly blind; but he recognized old friends by their voices, and was full of simple joy at meeting them.

"I have a very wonderful invention," he said, in his eager voice, his blind eyes wide and luminous; "and very valuable.

But I have not been financially successful, so far. I shall be, of course. But in the city no one seemed willing to wait for payment for my board, so the authorities advised me to come home; and, in fact, assisted me to do so. But when I finish my invention, I shall have ample means."

Jonesville, lounging on the porch of Dyer's Hotel, grinned, and said, "That's all right, Nat; you'll be a rich man one of these days!" And then it tapped its forehead significantly, and whispered, "Too bad!" and added (with ill-concealed pleasure at finding new misfortune to talk about) that the Selectmen had told Mr. Dean, the superintendent, that he could call at Dyer's Hotel—to which Nathaniel, peacefully and pennilessly, had drifted—and take him out to the Farm.

"Sam Dyer says he'll keep him till next week," Mrs. Butterfield told Lizzie Graham; "but, course, he can't just let him set down at the hotel for the rest of his natural life. And Nat May would do it, you know."

"I believe he would," Lizzie Graham admitted; "he was always kind of simple that way, willin' to take and willin' to give. Don't you mind how he used to be always sharin' anything he had? James used to say Nat never knowed his own things belonged to him."

"Folks like that don't never get rich," Mrs. Butterfield said; "but there! you like 'em."

The two women were walking down a stony hillside, each with a lard-pail full of blueberries. It was a hot August afternoon; a northwest wind, harsh and dry, tore fiercely across the scrub-pines and twinkling birches of the sun-baked pastures. Lizzie Graham held on to her sun-bonnet, and stopped in a scrap of shade under a meagre oak to get breath.

"My! I don't like wind," she said, laughing.

"Let's set down a while," Mrs. Butterfield suggested.

"I'd just as leaves," Lizzie said, and took off her blue sunbonnet and fanned herself. She was a pretty woman still, though she was nearly fifty; her hair was russet red, and blew about her forehead in little curls; her eyes, brown like a brook in shady places, and kind. It was a mild face, but not weak. Below them the valley shimmered in the heat; the grass was hot and brittle underfoot; popples bent and twisted in a scorching wind, and a soft, dark glitter of movement ran through the pines on the opposite hillside.

"The Farm ain't got a mite of shade round it," Lizzie said; "just sets there at the crossroads and bakes."

"You was always great for trees," Mrs. Butterfield said; "your house is too dark for my taste. If I was you, I'd cut down that biggest ellum."

"Cut it down! Well, I suppose you'll laugh, but them trees are real kind o' friends. There! I knowed you'd laugh; but I wouldn't cut down a tree any more 'an I'd—I don't know what!"

"They do darken."

"Some. But only in summer; and then you want 'em to. And the Poor Farm ain't got a scrap of shade!—I wonder if he feels it, bein' sent there?"

"I ain't seen, him, but Josh, told me he was terrible broke up over it. Told me he just set and wrung his hands when Hiram Wells told him he'd got to go. Josh said it was real pitiful. But what can you do? He's 'bout blind; and he ain't just right, either."

"How ain't he just right?"

"Well, you know, Nathaniel was always one of the dreamin'
kind; a real good man, but he wa'n't like folks."

Lizzie nodded.

"And if you remember, he was all the time inventin' things.
Well, now he's got set that he can invent a machine so as you
can see the dead. I mean spirits. Well, of course he's crazy.
Josh says he's crazy as a bluefish. But what's troublin' him
now is that he can't finish his machine. He says that if he
goes to the Farm, what with him bein' blindish and not able
to do for himself, that his glasses and wheels—and dear
knows what all that he's got for ghost-seein'—will get all
smashed up. An' I guess he's 'bout right. They're terrible
crowded, Mis' Dean says. Nat allows that if he could stay at
Dyer's, or some place, a couple of months, where he could
work, quiet, he'd make so much money that he'd pay his
board ten times over. Crazy. But then, I can't help bein' sorry
for him. Some folks don't mind the troubles of crazy folks,
but I don't know why they ain't as hard to bear as sensible
folks' troubles."

"Harder maybe," Lizzie said.

"Josh said he just set and wrung his hands together, and he
says to Hiram Wells, he says, 'Gimme a month—and I'll
finish it. For the sake,' he says, 'of the blessed dead.' Gave
you goose-flesh, Josh said."

"You can see that he believes in his machine."

"Oh, he's just as sure as he's alive!"

"But why can't he finish it at the Farm? I guess Mis' Dean would give him a closet to keep it in."

"Closet? Mercy! He's got it all spread out on a table in his room at the hotel. Them loafers go up and look at it, and bust right out laughin'. Josh says it's all little wheels and lookin'-glasses, and they got to be balanced just so. Mis' Dean ain't got a spot he could have for ten minutes at a time."

They were silent for a few minutes, and then Lizzie Graham said: "Does he feel bad at bein' a pauper? The Mays was always respectable. Old Mis' May was real proud."

Mrs. Butterfield ruminated: "Well, he don't like it, course. But he said (you know he's crazy)—'I am nothin',' he says, 'and my pride is less than nothin'. But for the sake of the poor Dead, grant me time,' he says. Ain't it pitiful? Almost makes you feel like lettin' him wait. But what's the use?"

Lizzie Graham nodded. "But there's people would pay money for one of them machines—if it worked."

"That's what he said; he said he'd make a pile of money. But he didn't care about that, except then he could pay board to Dyer, if Dyer'd let him stay."

"An' won't he?"

"No; and I don't see as he has any call to, any more 'an you or me."

Lizzie Graham plucked at the dry grass at her side. "That's so. 'Tain't one person's chore more 'an another's. But—there! If this wa'n't Jonesville, I believe I'd let him stay with me till he finishes up his machine."

"Why, Lizzie Graham!" cried Mrs. Butterfield, "what you talkin' about? You couldn't do it—you. You ain't got to spare, in the first place. And anyway, him an unmarried man, and you a widow woman! Besides, he'll never finish it."

Lizzie's face reddened angrily. "Guess I could have a visitor as well as anybody."

"Oh, I didn't mean you wouldn't be a good provider," Mrs. Butterfield said, turning red herself. "I meant folks would talk."

"Folks could find something better to talk about," Lizzie said; "Jonesville is just nothin' but a nest o' real mean, lyin' gossip!"

"Well, that's so," Mrs. Butterfield agreed, placidly.

Lizzie Graham put on her sunbonnet. "Better be gettin' along," she said.

Mrs. Butterfield rose ponderously. "And they'd say you was a spiritualist, too; they'd say you took him to get his ghost-machine made."

"That's just what I would do," the other answered, sharply. "I ain't a mite of a spiritualist, and I don't believe in ghosts; but I believe in bein' kind."

"I believe in keepin' a good name," Mrs. Butterfield said, dryly.

They went on down the windy pasture slope in silence; the mullein candles blossomed shoulder-high, and from under-foot came the warm, aromatic scent of sweet-fern. Once they stopped for some more blueberries, with a desultory word about the heat; then they picked their way around juniper-bushes, and over great knees of granite, hot and slippery, and through low, sweet thickets of bay. At the foot of the hill the shadows were stretching across the road, and the wind was flagging.

"My, ain't the shade good?" Lizzie said, when they stopped under her great elm; "I couldn't bear to live where there wa'n't trees."

"There's always shade on one side or another of the Poor Farm, anyway," Mrs. Butterfield said, "'cept at noon. And then he could set indoors. It won't be anything so bad, Lizzie. Now don't you get to worryin' 'bout him;—I know you, Lizzie Graham!" she ended, her eyes twinkling.

Lizzie took off her sunbonnet again and fanned herself; she looked at her old neighbor anxiously.

"Say, now, Mis' Butterfield, honest: do you think folks would talk?"

"If you took Nat in and kep' him? Course they would! You know they would; you know this here town. And no wonder they'd talk. You're a nice-appearin' woman, Lizzie, yet. No; I ain't one to flatter; you *be*. And ain't he a man? and a likely man, too, for all he's crazy. Course they'd talk! Now, Lizzie, don't you get to figgerin' on this. It's just like you! How many cats have you got on your hands now? I bet you're feedin' that lame dog yet."

Mrs. Graham laughed, but would not say.

"Nat will get along at the Farm real good, after he gets used to it," Mrs. Butterfield went on, coaxingly; "Dean ain't hard. And Mis' Dean's many a time told me what a good table they set."

"'Tain't the victuals that would trouble Nat May."

"Well, Lizzie, now you promise me you won't think anything more about him visitin' you?" Mrs. Butterfield looked at her anxiously.

"I guess Jonesville knows me, after I've lived here all my life!" Lizzie said, evasively.

"Knows you?" Mrs. Butterfield said; "what's that got to do with it? You know Jonesville; that's more to the point."

"It's a mean place!" Lizzie said, angrily.

"I'm not sayin' it ain't," Mrs. Butterfield agreed. "Well, Lizzie, you're good, but you ain't real sensible," she ended, affectionately.

Lizzie laughed, and swung her gate shut. She stood leaning on it a minute, looking after Mrs. Butterfield laboriously climbing the hill, until the road between its walls of rusty hazel-bushes and its fringe of joepye-weed and goldenrod turned to the left and the stout, kindly figure disappeared. The great elm moved softly overhead, and Lizzie glanced up through its branches, all hung with feathery twigs, at the deep August sky.

"Jonesville's never talked about *me*!" she said to herself, proudly. "I mayn't be wealthy, but I got a good name. Course it wouldn't do to take Nat; but my! ain't it a poor planet where you can't do a kind act?"

II

Nathaniel May sat in his darkness, brooding over his machine. Since it had been definitely arranged that he was to go to the Poor Farm, he did not care how soon he went; there was no need, he told Dyer, to keep him for the few days which had been promised.

"I had thought," he said, patiently, "that some one would take me in and help me finish my machine—for the certain profit that I could promise them. But nobody seems to believe in me," he ended.

"Oh, folks believe in you, all right, Mr. May," Dyer told him; "but they don't believe in your machine. See?"

Nathaniel's face darkened. "Blind—blind!" he said.

"How did it come on you?" Dyer asked, sympathetically.

"I was not speaking of myself," Nathaniel told him, hopelessly.

There was really no doubt that the poor, gentle mind had staggered under the weight of hope; but it was hardly more than a deepening of old vagueness, an intensity of absorbed thought upon unpractical things. The line between sanity and insanity is sometimes a very faint one; no one can quite dare to say just when it has been crossed. But this mild creature had crossed it somewhere in the beginning of his certainty that he was going to give the world the means of seeing the unseen. That this great gift should be flung into oblivion, all for the want, as he believed, of a little time, broke his poor heart. When Lizzie Graham came to see him, she found him sitting in his twilight, his elbows on his knees, his head in his long, thin hands. On one hollow cheek there was a glistening wet streak. He put up a forlornly trembling hand and wiped it away when he heard her voice.

"Yes; yes, I do recognize it, ma'am," he said; "I can tell voices better than I used to be able to tell faces. You are Jim Graham's wife? Yes; yes, Lizzie Graham. Have you heard about me, Lizzie? I am not going to finish my machine. I am to be sent to the Farm."

"Yes, I heard," she said.

They were in the big, bare office of the hotel. The August sunshine lay dim upon the dingy window-panes; the walls, stained by years of smoke and grime, were hidden by yellowing advertisements of reapers and horse liniments; in the centre was a dirty iron stove. A poor, gaunt room, but a haven to Nathaniel May, awaiting the end of hope.

"I heard," Lizzie Graham said; she leaned forward and stroked his hand. "But maybe you can finish it at the Farm, Nathaniel?"

"No," he said, sadly; "no; I know what it's like at the Farm. There is no room there for anything but bodies. No time for anything but Death."

"How long would it take you to put it together?" she asked; and Dyer, who was lounging across his counter, shook his head at her, warningly.

"There ain't nothin' to it, Mrs. Graham," he said, under his breath; "he's—" He tapped his forehead significantly.

"Oh, man!" Nathaniel cried out, passionately, "you don't know what you say! Are the souls of the departed 'nothing'? I have it in my hand—right here in my hand, Lizzie Graham—to give the world the gift of sight. And they won't give me a crust of bread and a roof over my head till I can offer it to them!"

"Couldn't somebody put it together for you?" she asked, the tears in her eyes. "I would try, Nathaniel;—you could explain it to me; I could come and see you every day, and you could tell me."

His face brightened into a smile. "No, kind woman. Only I can do it. I can't see very clearly, but there is a glimmer of light, enough to get it together. But it would take at least two months; at least two months. The doctor said the light would last, perhaps, three months. Then I shall be blind. But if I could give eyes to the blind world before I go into the dark, what matter? What matter, I say?" he cried, brokenly.

Lizzie was silent. Dyer shook his head, and tapped his forehead again; then he lounged out from behind his counter, and settled himself in one of the armchairs outside the office door.

Nathaniel dropped his head upon his breast, and sunk back into his dreams. The office was very still, except for two bluebottle flies butting against the ceiling and buzzing up and down the window-panes. A hot wind wandered in and flapped a mowing-machine poster on the wall; then dropped, and the room was still again, except that leaf shadows moved across the square of sunshine on the bare boards by the open door. When Lizzie got up to go, he did not hear her kind good-by until she repeated it, touching his shoulder with her friendly hand. Then he said, hastily, with a faint frown: "Good-by. Good-by." And sank again into his daze of disappointment.

Lizzie wiped her eyes furtively before she went out upon the hotel porch; there Dyer, balancing comfortably on two legs of his chair, detained her with drawling gossip until Hiram Wells came up, and, lounging against a zinc-sheathed bar between two hitching-posts, added his opinion upon Nathaniel May's affairs.

"Well, Lizzie, seen any ghosts?" he began.

"I seen somebody that'll be a ghost pretty soon if you send him off to the Farm," Lizzie said, sharply.

"Well," Hiram said, "I don't see what's to be done—'less some nice, likely woman comes along and marries him."

Dyer snickered. Lizzie turned very red, and started home down the elm-shaded street. When she reached her little gray house under its big tree, she went first into the cow-barn—a crumbling lean-to with a sagging roof—to see if a sick dog which had found shelter there was comfortable. It seemed to Lizzie that his bleared eyes should be washed; and she did this before she went through her kitchen into a shed-room where she slept. There she sat down in hurried and frowning preoccupation, resting her elbows on her knees and staring blankly at the braided mat on the floor. As she sat there her face reddened; and once she laughed, nervously. "An' me 'most fifty!" she said to herself....

The next morning she went to see Nathaniel again.

He was up-stairs in a little hot room under the sloping eaves. He was bending over, straining his poor eyes close to some small wheels and bands and reflectors arranged on a shaky table. He welcomed her eagerly, and with all the excitement of conviction plunged at once into an explanation of his principle. Then suddenly conviction broke into despair: "I am not to be allowed to finish it!" He gave a quick sob, like a child. He had forgotten Lizzie's presence.

"Nathaniel," she said, and paused; then began again: "Nathaniel—"

"Who is here? Oh yes: Lizzie Graham. Kind woman; kind woman."

"Nathaniel, you know I ain't got means; I'm real poor,—"

"Are you?" he said, with instant concern. "I am sorry. If I could help you—if I had anything of my own—or if they will let me finish my machine; then I shall have all the money I want, and I will help you; I will give you all you need. I will give to all who ask!" he said, joyfully; then again, abruptly: "But no; but no; I am not allowed to finish it."

"Nathaniel, what I was going to say was—I am real poor. I got James's pension, and our house out on the upper road;— do you mind it—a mite of a house, with a big elm right by the gate? And woods on the other side of the road? Real shady and pleasant. And I got eight hens and a cow;—well, she'll come in in September, and I'll have real good milk all winter. Maybe this time I could raise the calf, if it's a heifer. Generally I sell it; but if you—well, it might pay to raise it, if—we—" Lizzie stammered with embarrassment.

Nathaniel had forgotten her again; his head had fallen forward on his breast, and he sighed heavily.

"You see, I *am* poor," Lizzie said; "you wouldn't have comforts."

Nathaniel was silent.

Lizzie laughed, nervously. "Well? Seems queer; but—will you?"

Nathaniel, waking from his troubled dream, said, patiently: "What did you say? I ask your pardon; I was not listening."

"Why," Lizzie said, her face very red, "I was just saying— if—if you didn't mind getting married, Nathaniel, you could come and live with me?"

"Married?" he said, vacantly. "To whom?"

"Me," she said.

Nathaniel turned toward her in astonishment. "Married!" he repeated.

"If you lived with me, you could finish the machine; there's an attic over my house; I guess it's big enough. Only, we'd *have* to be married, I'm afraid. Jonesville is a mean place, Nathaniel. We'd have to be married. But you could finish the machine."

He stood up, trembling, the tears suddenly running down his face. *"Finish it?"* he said, in a whisper. "Oh, you are not deceiving me? You would not deceive me?"

"I don't see why you couldn't finish it," she told him, kindly. "But, Nathaniel, mind, I am poor. You wouldn't get as good victuals even as you would at the Farm. And you'd have to marry me, or folks would talk about me. But you could finish your machine."

Nathaniel lifted his dim eyes to heaven.

III

"Well," said Mrs. Butterfield, "I suppose you know your own business. But my goodness sakes alive!"

"I just thought I'd tell you," Lizzie said.

"But, Lizzie Graham! you ain't got the means."

"I can feed him."

"There's his clothes; why, my land—"

"I told Hiram Wells that if the town would see to his clothes, I'd do the rest. They'd have to clothe him if he went to the Farm."

"Well," said Mrs. Butterfield, "I never in all my born days—Lizzie, now *don't*. My goodness,—I—I ain't got no words! Why, his victuals—"

"He ain't hearty. Sam Dyer told me he wa'n't hearty."

"Well, then, Sam Dyer had better feed him, 'stid o' puttin' it onto you!"

Lizzie was silent. Then she said, with a short sigh, "Course if I could 'a' just taken him in an' kep' him—but you said folks would talk—"

"Well, I guess so. Course they'd talk—you know this place. You've always been well thought of in Jonesville, but that would 'a' been the end of you, far as bein' respectable goes."

"Well, you can't say this ain't respectable."

"No; I can't say it ain't respectable; but I can say it's the foolishest thing I ever heard of. An' wrong too; 'cause anything foolish is wrong."

"Anything cruel is wrong," Lizzie said, stubbornly.

"Well, you was crazy to think of havin' him visit you. But it don't follow, 'cause he can't be visitin' you, that you got to go *marry* him."

"I got to do something," Lizzie said, desperately; "I'd never have a minute's peace if he had to go to the Farm."

"He'd be more comfortable there."

"His stomach might be," Lizzie admitted.

"Well, then!" Mrs. Butterfield declared, triumphantly. "Now you just let him go, Lizzie. You just be sensible."

"I'm goin' to marry him. I'm goin' to take him round to Rev. Niles day after to-morrow; he said he'd marry us."

Mrs. Butterfield gasped. "Well, if Rev. Niles does that!— There! You know he was a 'Piscopal; they'll do anything. What did he say when you told him?"

"Oh, nothin' much; I asked him about him visitin' me, an' he said it wa'n't just customary. Said it was better to get married. Said we must avoid the appearance of evil."

"Well, I ain't sayin' he ain't right; but—" Then, in despair, she turned to ridicule: "Folks'll say you're marryin' him 'cause you expect he'll make money on his ghost-machine!"

"Well, you tell 'em I don't believe in ghosts. That'll settle *that*."

"If folks knew you didn't believe in any hereafter, they'd say you was a wicked woman!" cried Mrs. Butterfield, angrily;—"an' that fool machine—"

"I never said I didn't believe in a hereafter. Course his machine ain't sense. That's what makes it so pitiful."

"He'll never finish it."

"Course he won't. That's why I'm takin' him."

"Well, my *sakes!*" said Mrs. Butterfield, helplessly. And then, angrily again, "Course if you set out to go your own way, I suppose you don't expect no help from them as thinks you are all wrong?"

"I do not," Lizzie said, steadily; and then a spark glinted in her leaf-brown eye: "Folks that have means, and yet would let that poor unfortunate be taken to the Farm—I wouldn't expect no help from 'em."

"Well, Mis' Graham, you can't say I ain't warned you."

"No, Mis' Butterfield, I can't," Lizzie responded; and the two old friends parted stiffly.

The word that Lizzie Graham—"poor as Job's turkey!"—was going to marry Nathaniel May spread like grass fire through Jonesville. Mrs. Butterfield preserved a cold silence, for her distress was great. To hear people snicker and say that Lizzie Graham must be "dyin' anxious to get married"; that she must be "lottin' considerable on a good ghost-market"; that she "took a new way o' gettin' a hired man without payin' no wages,"—these things stung her sore heart into actual anger at the friend she loved. But she did not show it.

"Mis' Graham probably knows her own business," she said, stiffly, to any one who spoke to her of the matter. Even to her own husband she was non-committal. Josh sat out by the kitchen door, tilting back against the gray-shingled side of the house, his hands in his pockets, his feet tucked under him on the rung of his chair. He was in his shirt-sleeves, and he had unbuttoned his baggy old waistcoat, for it was a hot night. Mrs. Butterfield was on the kitchen door-step. They could look across a patch of grass at the great barn, connected with the little house by a shed. Its doors were still open, and Josh could see the hay, put in that afternoon. The rick in the yard stood like a skeleton against the fading yellow of the sky; some fowls were roosting comfortably on the tongue. It was very peaceful; but Mrs. Butterfield's face was puckered with anxiety. "Yet I don't know as I can do anything about it," she said, her foot tapping the stone step nervously; "she ain't got no call to be so foolish."

"Well," Josh said, removing his pipe from his lips and spitting thoughtfully, "seems Mis' Graham's bound to get some kind of a husband!" Then he chuckled, and thrust his pipe back under his long, shaven upper lip.

"Now look a-here, Josh Butterfield; you don't want to be talkin' that way," his wife said, bitterly. "Bad enough to have folks that don't know no better pokin' fun at her; but I ain't a-goin' to have you do it."

"Well, I was only just sayin'—"

"Well, don't you say it; that's all."

Josh poked a gnarled thumb down into the bowl of his pipe, reflectively. "You ain't got a match about you, have you, Emmy?" he said, coaxingly.

Mrs. Butterfield rose and went into the kitchen to get the match; when she handed it to him, she said, sighing, "I'm just 'most sick over it."

"You do seem consid'able shuck up," Josh said, kindly.

"Well,—I know Lizzie's just doin' it out of pure goodness; but she'll 'most starve."

"I don't see myself how she's calculatin' to run things," Josh ruminated; "course Jim's pension wa'n't much, but it was somethin'. And without it—"

"Without it?—land! Is the government goin' to stop pensions? There! I never did like the President!"

"No; the government ain't goin' to stop it. Lizzie Graham's goin' to stop it."

"What on airth you talkin' about?"

"Why, Emmy woman, don't ye know the United States government ain't no such fool as to go on payin' a woman for havin' a dead husband when she catches holt of a livin' one? Don't you know that?"

"Josh Butterfield!—you don't mean—"

"Why, that's true. Didn't you know that? Well, well! Why, a smart widow woman could get consid'able of a income by sendin' husbands to wars, if it wa'n't for that. Well, well; to think you didn't know that! Wonder if Lizzie does?"

"She don't!" Mrs. Butterfield said, excitedly; "course she don't. She's calculatin' on havin' that pension same as ever.

Why, she *can't* marry Nat. Goodness! I guess I'll just step down and tell her. Lucky you told me to-night; to-morrow it would 'a' been too late!"

IV

Lizzie Graham was sitting in the dark on her door-step; a cat had curled up comfortably in her lap; her elm was faintly murmurous with a constant soft rustling and whispering of the lace of leaves around its great boughs. Now and then a tree-toad spoke, or from the pasture pond behind the house came the metallic twang of a bullfrog. But nothing else broke the deep stillness of the summer night. Lizzie's elbow was on her knee, her chin in her hand; she was listening to the peace, and thinking—not anxiously, but seriously. After all, it was a great undertaking: Nathaniel wasn't "hearty," perhaps,—but when you don't average four eggs a day (for in November and December the hens do act like they are possessed!); when sometimes your cow will be dry; when your neighbor is mad and won't remember the potato-barrel—the outlook for one is not simple; for two it is sobering.

"But I can do it," Lizzie said to herself, and set her lips hard together.

The gate clicked shut, and Mrs. Butterfield came in, running almost. "Look here, Lizzie Graham,—oh my! wait till I get my breath;—*Lizzie, you can't do it.* Because—" And then, panting, she explained. "So, you see, you just can't," she repeated.

Lizzie said something under her breath, and stared with blank bewilderment at her informant.

"Maybe Josh don't know?"

"Maybe he does know," retorted Mrs. Butterfield. "Goodness! makes me tremble to think if he hadn't told me to-night! Supposin' he hadn't let on about it till this time to-morrow?"

Lizzie put her hands over her face with an exclamation of dismay.

"Oh, well, there!" Mrs. Butterfield said, comfortably; "I don't believe Nat'll mind after he's been at the Farm a bit. Honest, I don't, Lizzie. How comes it you didn't know yourself?"

"I'm sure I don't know; it ain't on my certificate, anyhow. Maybe it's on the voucher; but I ain't read that since I first went to sign it. I just go every three months and draw my money, and think no more about it. Maybe—if they knew at Washington—"

"Sho! they couldn't make a difference for one; and it's just what Josh says—they ain't goin' to pay you for havin' a dead husband if you got a live one. Well, it wouldn't be sense, Lizzie."

Lizzie shook her head. "Wait till I look at my paper—"

Mrs. Butterfield followed her into the house, and waited while she lighted a lamp and lifted a blue china vase off the shelf above the stove. "I keep it in here," Lizzie said, shaking the paper out. Then, unfolding it on the kitchen table, the two women, the lamplight shining upon their excited faces, read the certificate together, aloud, with agitated voices:

"BUREAU OF PENSIONS

"It is hereby certified that in conformity with the laws of the United States—" and on through to the end.

"It don't say a word about not marryin' again," Lizzie declared.

"Well, all the same, it's the law. Josh knows."

Lizzie blew out the lamp, and they went back to the doorstep. Mrs. Butterfield's hard feelings were all gone; her heart warmed to Nathaniel; warmed even to the mangy dog that limped out from the barn and curled up on Lizzie's skirt. But when she went away, "comfortable in her mind," as she told her husband, Lizzie Graham still sat in the dark under her elm, trying to get her wits together.

"I know Josh is right," she told herself; "he's a careful talker. I can't do it!" But she winced, and drew in her breath; poor Nathaniel!

She had seen him that afternoon, and had told him, this time with no embarrassment (for he was as simple as a child about it), that she had arranged with Mr. Niles to marry them. "An' you fetch your bag along, Nathaniel, and we'll put the machine together, evenin's," she said.

"Yes, kind woman," he answered, joyously. "Oh, what a weight you have taken from my soul!"

His half-blind eyes were luminous with belief. Lizzie had smiled, and shaken her head slightly, looking at the battered rubbish in the bag—the little, tarnished mirrors, one of them cracked; the two small lenses, scratched and dim; the handful of rusty cogs and wheels. With what passion he had dreamed that he would see that which it hath not entered into the heart of man to conceive! He began to talk, eagerly, of his invention; but reasonably, it seemed to Lizzie. Indeed, except for the idea itself, there was nothing that betrayed the unbalanced mind. His gratitude, too, was sane enough; he had been planning how he could he useful to her, how he was to do this or that sort of work for her—at least until his eyes gave out, he said, cheerfully. "But by that time, kind woman, my invention will be perfected, and you shall have no need to consider ways and means."

Lizzie, smiling, had left him to his joy, and gone back to sit under her elm in the twilight, and think soberly of the economies which a husband—such a husband—would necessitate.

And then Mrs. Butterfield had come panting up to the gate; and now—

"I don't see as I can tell him!" she thought, desperately. To go and say to Nathaniel, all eager and happy and full of hope as he was, "You must go to the Farm,"—would be like striking in the face some child that is holding out its arms to you. Lizzie twisted her hands together. "I just can't!" But, of course, she would have to. That was all there was to it. If she married him, why, there would be two to go to the Farm instead of one. Oh, why wouldn't they give her her pension if she married again! Her eyes smarted with tears; Nathaniel's pain seemed to her unendurable.

But all the same, the next morning, heavily, she set out to tell him.

At Dyer's, Jonesville had gathered to see the sight; and as she came up to the porch, there were nudgings and whisperings, and Hiram Wells, bolder than the rest, said, "Well, Mis' Graham, this is a fine day for a weddin'—"

Lizzie Graham, without turning her head, said, coldly, "There ain't goin' to be no weddin'." Then she went on upstairs to Nathaniel's room.

The idlers on the porch looked at each other and guffawed. "I knowed Sam was foolin' us," somebody said.

But Sam defended himself. "I tell you I wa'n't foolin'. You ask Rev. Niles; she told me only yesterday he said he'd tie the knot. I ain't foolin'. She's changed her mind, that's all."

"Lookin' for a handsomer man," Hiram suggested;—"chance for yourself, Sam!"

Lizzie, hot-cheeked, heard the laughter, and went on up-stairs. Nathaniel was sitting on the edge of his bed, his hat on, his poor coat buttoned to his chin; he was holding his precious bag, gripped in two nervous hands, on his knee. When he heard her step, he drew a deep breath.

"Oh, kind woman!" he said; "I'd begun to fear you were not coming."

"I am—a little late," Lizzie said. "I—I was detained."

"It does not matter," he said, cheerfully; "I have had much food for thought while awaiting you. I have been thinking that this wonderful invention will be really your gift to humanity, not mine. Had I gone to the Farm, it would never have been. Now—!" His voice broke for joy.

"Oh, well, I don't know 'bout that," Lizzie said, nervously; "I guess you could 'a' done it anywheres."

"No, no; it would have been impossible. And think, Lizzie Graham, what it will mean to the sorrowful world! See," he explained, solemnly; "we poor creatures have not been able to conceive that of which we have had no experience; the unborn child cannot know the meaning of life. If the babe in the womb questioned, What is birth? what is living? could even its own mother tell it? Nay! So we, questioning: 'God, what is death? what is immortality?' Not even God can tell us. The unborn soul, carried in the womb of Time, has waited death to know the things of Eternity, just as the unborn babe waits birth to know the things of life. But now,

now, is coming to the world the gift of sight!"

There was a pause; Lizzie Graham swallowed once, and set her lips; then she said, "I am afraid, Nathaniel, that I—I can't marry you—because—"

"Marry me?" he said, with a confused look.

"We were to get married to-day, you know, Nathaniel?"

"Oh yes," he said.

"Yes; but—but I can't, Nathaniel."

"Never mind," he said. "Shall we go now, kind woman?" He rose, smiling, and stretched out one groping hand. Involuntarily she took it; then stood still, and tried to speak. He turned patiently towards her. "Must we wait longer?" he asked, gently.

"Oh, Nathaniel, I—I don't know what to say, but—"

A startled look came into his face. "Is anything the matter?"

"*Oh!*" Lizzie said. "It just breaks my heart!"

His face turned suddenly gray; he sat down, trembling; the contents of his bag rattled, and something snapped—perhaps another mirror broke. He put one hand up to his head.

"It's that pension," Lizzie said, brokenly; "if I get married, I lose it. An' we wouldn't have a cent to live on. You—you see how it is, Nathaniel?"

He began to whisper to himself, not listening to her. There was a long pause, broken by his strange whispering.

Lizzie Graham looked at him, and turned her eyes away, wincing with pain;—the tears were rolling slowly down his cheeks. She put her hand on his shoulder in a passion of pity; then, suddenly, fiercely, she gathered the poor bowed head against her soft breast. "I don't care! My name ain't worth as much as that! Let 'em talk. Nathaniel, are you willin' *not* to get married?"

But she had to speak twice before he heard her. Then he said, looking up at her out of his despair: "What? What did you say?"

"Nathaniel," she explained, kneeling beside him and holding his hand against her bosom, "if you were to come and live with me, and we were not married—"

But he was not listening. A door opened down-stairs, and there was a noisy burst of laughter; then it closed, and the hot room was still.

"Emily Butterfield will stand my friend," she said, her lips tightening. Then, gently: "We won't get married; Nathaniel. You will just come and visit me until—until the machine is finished."

"You will let me come?" he said, with a gasp; "you will let me finish my invention?" He got up, trembling, clutching his bag, and holding out one hand to clasp hers.

Lizzie Graham took it, and stood stock-still for one hard moment....

Then she led him down-stairs, out upon the porch, past the loafers gaping and nudging each other.

"Goin' to be married, after all, Mis' Graham?" some one said.

And Lizzie Graham turned and faced them. "No," she said, calmly.

Then they went out into the sunshine together.

"AND ANGELS CAME—"

BY ANNE O'HAGAN

The full effulgence of cloudless midsummer enveloped the place. The lawns, bright and soft, sloped for half a mile to the sweetbrier hedge. Among them wound the drive, now and again crossing the stone bridges of the small, curving lake which gave the estate its affected name—Lakeholm. To the left of the house a coppice of bronze beeches shone with dark lustre; clumps of rhododendrons enlivened the green with splashes of color. Lombardy poplars, with their gibbetlike erectness, bordered the roads and intersected them with mathematical shadows; here and there rose a feathery elm or a maple of wide-branched beauty. To the right, a shallow fall of terraces led to the Italian garden, Mrs. Dinsmore's chief pride, now a glory of matched and patterned color and a dazzle of spray from marble basins. Beyond all the careful, exotic beauty of the place, the wide valley dipped away, alternate meadow and grove, until it met the silvery shiver of willows marking the course of the river. Beyond that again, the hills, solemn in unbroken green, rose to cloud-touched heights.

Before the house Brockton's new automobile waited. He himself leaned against a stone pillar of the piazza, facing his hostess, who sat on the edge of a chair in the tense attitude of protest against delay. She had scarcely recovered from her waking crossness yet, and found herself more irritated than amused at the eccentricities of her guest. She was wondering with unusual asperity why a man with such lack-lustre blue eyes dared to wear a tie of such brilliant contrast. He interrupted her musings.

"Miss Harned seems mighty stand-offish these days."

"Millicent is a little difficult," admitted Millicent's cousin.

"What do you suppose it is? She seemed all smooth enough in New York last winter, and even in the spring after—But now—" He paused again without finishing his sentence. "And I had counted on your influence to make her more approachable."

"Oh, Millicent is having a struggle with her better nature, that is all," laughed Mrs. Dinsmore. "It's hard living with her during the process, but she's adorable once her noble impulses have been vanquished and she's comfortably like the rest of the world again."

"I don't know what you mean," said the downright Mr. Brockton.

"No?" Mrs. Dinsmore was sure that the impertinence of her monosyllable would be lost upon her elderly protege. "I'll make it clear to you, if I can. Millicent, you know, has nothing—"

"With that figure and that face?" interrupted Brockton, with gallant enthusiasm.

"I was speaking in your terms, Mr. Brockton," said the lady, with suave hauteur. "Of course all of us count my cousin's charm and accomplishments, though we do not inventory them as possessions far above rubies. But in the valuation of the 'change she has nothing. Oh, she may manage to extract five or six hundred a year from some investments of my uncle, and she has the old Harned place in New Hampshire. That might bring in as much as seven hundred dollars if the abandoned farm-fever were still on—"

"By ginger!" boasted Brockton, whose expletives lacked *ton*, "it's more than I had when I started."

"So I remember your saying before. But I fear that my cousin is not a financial genius. What I meant by her struggles with her better nature is that she sometimes tries to thwart us when we want to make things easy for her. Her better nature had a fearful tussle with her common sense about five years ago, when Aunt Jessie asked her to go abroad; and it nearly overcame her frivolity and her vanity last winter when I met her at the dock and insisted upon having her spend the winter with me, and our second cousin, Alicia Broome, offered to be responsible for her wardrobe. But, thanks be," she added, laughing, "the world, the flesh, and the devil won. So cheer up, Mr. Brockton. It may happen again."

"Oh, I'm not hopeless by any manner of means. I want her pretty badly, and I'm used to getting what I want. I told her, out and out, when she turned me down, back there in May, that if she were a young girl I wouldn't urge her any more, after what she said about her feelings. But she wasn't, and I thought she could look at a proposition from a plain business point of view."

"You told her that? You mentioned to her that she was no longer a young girl?" Mrs. Dinsmore's laugh rippled delightedly on the air.

"I did. Oh, I'm used to bargaining," he rejoined, proudly. "I always could make the other fellow see what he'd lose by refusing my offers. And I got her to take the matter under consideration. I heard somewhere that she was interested in some philanthropy. Well, money comes in handy in charity." He grinned broadly at Mrs. Dinsmore.

At that moment her protege was extremely distasteful to the lady. But she was a philosopher where marriage was concerned, and she whole-heartedly hoped that her cousin Millicent would not dally too long with her opportunity and allow the matrimonial prize to escape. She was sincerely fond of Millicent, and desired for her the best things in the world. She sometimes said so with touching earnestness.

"She told me"—Mr. Brockton stumbled slightly—"that there wasn't any one else."

"There isn't. She has her train—she's enormously admired—but there is no one in whom she is sentimentally interested. And Aunt Jessie says it was so all the time they were in Europe."

"Wasn't there ever?" he demanded.

"My dear Mr. Brockton, Millicent is twenty-nine, as you reminded her, and she's a normal woman! Of course there have been some ones—her music-master at fourteen, I dare say, and an actor at sixteen, and a young curate at eighteen—oh, of course I'm jesting. But I suppose she was somewhat like other girls. She was engaged at nineteen—and he must have been quite twenty-three! No, I should dismiss all jealousy of her past if I were you."

"Engaged?"

Mrs. Dinsmore wondered suddenly if she had been wise, after all, to admit that widely known fact.

"Oh yes, a bread-and-butter engagement. My uncle was notoriously inadequate in all practical affairs; he was a scholar and something of a recluse and the most charming gentleman I ever saw, but a child in worldly matters,—a child! It ended, you see."

"How did it end?"

"Oh, poor Will Hayter died."

"Dead long?"

"Five or six years."

"Well, I'm not afraid of dead men." Brockton laughed in relief. Mrs. Dinsmore did not point out to him from her more subtle knowledge that constancy to the unchanging dead is sometimes easier than constancy to the variable living. She was only too glad to have the inevitable disclosure made lightly and the truth dismissed without frightening off the desirable suitor. "And certainly Miss Harned don't look as if, as if—"

"Any irremediable grief were gnawing at her damask cheeks?—"

"What's this about damask cheeks?" The question came along with a swirl of skirts from the great hall. "Cousin Anna, don't hate me for keeping you so long. Mr. Brockton, I owe you a thousand apologies."

Some of those who admitted Millicent Harned's charm declared that it lay in her voice. Always there sounded through its music the note of eagerness, with eagerness's underlying hint of pathos. Her tones were like her face, her motions, herself. Impulse, merriment, yearning, and the shadow of melancholy dwelt in her eyes and shaped her lips to sensitive curves. She was tall, and her motions were of a spontaneous grace, swifter and more changeful than most women's.

"You have been a disgracefully long time, Millicent," her cousin answered her apology. "But"—she looked at the beautifully gowned figure, the lovely, imaginative face, thereby, like a good showman, calling Mr. Brockton's attention to them—"we'll forgive you."

"Oh, it wasn't primping that kept me. I stopped for a few minutes at the schoolroom door. Poor Lena! She seemed to be feeling the responsibilities of erudition terribly this morning. She showed me her botany slides with such an air! Do you know what genus has the *rostellum*, Anna?"

"No, I don't," said Anna, shortly. "And Lena's growing up a perfect young prig. I'll have to change governesses. Heaven knows what I'll draw next time! The last one had charm, but no learning, and mighty little intelligence. This one has no manner at all, and is of encyclopaedic information. A daughter's a terrible responsibility."

"Isn't she?" Millicent's tone was one of affectionate raillery as she gathered her draperies about her in the automobile. The notion of Anna's responsibilities amused her; Anna was so untouched by them—as smooth-skinned, as slim and vivacious, as the forty-year-old mother of two boys entering college, a girl in the schoolroom and another in the nursery, as she had been as a *debutante*.

"Oh, you may make fun," said Anna, snapping open the

frothy thing she called a sunshade, "but you don't know how I lie awake nights, shuddering lest Lena grow up a near-sighted girl with no color and serious views."

Millicent only smiled as the great machine moved off. The sunshine, the rare and ordered beauty of the place, the fragrance of the soft winds, all lapped her in indolence. As they neared the gate that gave upon the open road, a turn brought them in sight of the front of the house. It was very beautiful. She breathed deeply in the content of the sight—the delicate lines, the soft color, the perfection of detail. In the gardens were stained, mellow columns and balustrades which Anna had brought from the dismantled palace in the Italian hills where she had found them. Everywhere wealth made its subtlest, most delicate appeal to her eyes.

"My house," thought Millicent, as they shot out of the grounds, "shall be different, but as beautiful. The Tudor style, I think, and for my out-of-door glory a vast rose-garden,—acres, if I please!" Then she called sternly to her straying imagination. She was picturing what she might have as the wife of the man before her—the man whose first proposal she had unhesitatingly refused, whose appearance at Lakeholm she had regarded as proof of disloyalty on Anna's part—the man who at the best represented to her only the artistic possibilities of riches. She dismissed her reverie with a frown and joined in the talk.

"Do you know," she confessed, "I forget where it is that we are going?"

"We're coming back to the Monroes' for luncheon," Mrs. Dinsmore reminded her. "But Mr. Brockton is going to skim over most of the Berkshires first. I think you said you hadn't been in this part of the country before, Mr. Brockton?"

"No," said Brockton, "I haven't had much chance to get acquainted with the playgrounds of the country. I've been too busy earning a holiday. But I've earned it all right." He turned to emphasize his boast with a nod toward Millicent. She blushed. His very chauffeur must redden at his braggart air, she thought. The Tudor castle grew dim in her vision.

"What do you think of the bubble, Miss Harned?" he went on. "Goes like a bird, don't she?"

"Indeed she does," answered Millicent, characteristically making immediate atonement in voice and look for the mental criticism of the moment before. "It's really going like a bird. I don't suppose we shall ever have a sensation more like flying."

"Not until our celestial pinions are adjusted," said Anna. Brockton laughed, but Millicent went on:

"Seriously, the loveliest belief I ever lost was the one in the wings with which my virtues should be at last rewarded. To breast the ether among the whirling stars,—didn't you ever lie awake and think of the possibility of that, Anna?"

"Never! I'm no poet in a state of suffocation, as I sometimes suspect you of being."

"As for heaven," declared Brockton, "I don't take much stock in all that. We're here—we know that—and we'd better make the most of it. For all we know, it's our last chance to have a good time. Better take all that's coming to you here and now, Miss Harned, and not count much on those wings of yours."

Millicent smiled mechanically. Could any Elizabethan garden of delight compensate for the misery of having each butterfly of fancy crushed between Lemuel Brockton's big hands in this fashion?

They were entering a village. Before them was the triangular green with the soldier's monument upon it. About it were the post-office, the stores, the small neat houses of the place. A white church, tall-steepled, green-shuttered, rose behind the monument, and with it dominated the square. A wagon or two toiled lazily along the road; before the stores a few dusty buggies were tied. The place seemed drowsy to stagnation in the summer heat. Why, Millicent wondered, were towns so crude and unlovely in the midst of a country so beautiful?

There was a sudden explosive sound, and, with a crunch and a jerk which almost threw them from their seats, the machine came to a standstill. Brockton and his chauffeur were out in an instant, the one peering beneath, the other examining more closely. He emerged in a moment, and there was a jargon of explanation, unintelligible to the two women. All that Anna and Millicent understood was that the accident was not serious; that they would be delayed only a few minutes, and that Brockton was very angry with some one for the mishap. The two men worked together. Anna looked at her cousin.

"I'm dead sleepy," she half whispered. "The wind in my face and the sun are too soporific for me. Let us not say a word to each other."

"You read last night," Millicent accused her. "But I don't feel particularly conversational myself."

She leaned back and surveyed the scene again. She could read the words graved on the granite block beneath the bronze soldier:

"To the men of Warren who fought that their country might

be whole and their fellows free this tribute of love is erected."

And there followed the honor-roll of Warren's fallen.

Millicent's sensitive lips quivered a little. Her ready imagination pictured them coming to this very square, perhaps,—the men of Warren. Boys from the hill farms, men from the village shops, the blacksmith who had worked in the light of yonder old forge, the carpenter who was father to the one now leisurely hammering a yellow L upon that weather-stained house,—she saw them all. What had led them? What call had sounded in their ears that they should leave their ploughshares in the furrows, their tills, their anvils, and their benches? What better thing had stirred with the primeval instinct for fight, with the unquenchable, restless longing for adventure, to send them forth? She read the words again—"that their country might be whole and their fellows free."

She moved impatiently. For now an old shadowy theory of hers—an inheritance from the theories of the recluse, her father—stirred from a long-drugged quiet: a theory that there was a disintegrating unpatriotism in the untouched, charmed life of riches she and her fellows sought. She felt the disturbing conviction that those common men—she could almost hear their blundering speech, see their uncouth yawns at the sights and sounds of beauty on which she fed her soul—that those men had wells of life within them purer, sweeter, than she. She averted her eyes from the monument.

"Honey!" called a voice, full-throated and loving—"honey, where are you?"

There was a play-tent on the little patch of yard before the brown cottage to the left. The voice had come from the narrow piazza. Millicent shivered as she looked at it, with its gingerbread decorations already succumbing to the strain of the seasons. The answer came from the tent:

"Here I am, muvver. Did you want me?"

She came out—a child of five or six years. The round-eyed solemnity of babyhood had not left her yet. She brought her small doll family with her, and a benevolent collie ambled beside her. Her mother watched, tenderness beautifying her brown eyes: she was a young woman, no older than Millicent, but her face was more lined than Anna's; a strand of dark hair was blown across her cheek; there were fruit stains on her apron. All the marks of a busy household life were about her, all the bounteous restfulness of a woman well beloved, and the anxieties of a loving woman. She gave the automobile a passing glance, but it had no interest for her. Her eyes came back to caress the young thing which toiled up the steps to her, babbling of a morning's events in the tent.

"Yes, sweetheart, that was very nice," she said, in answer to some breathless demand for sympathy. "And mother has brought you the bread and jam she promised you this morning. Will you eat it here, or in the tent?"

"Couldn't I come into the kitchen to eat it, where you are?"

"Why, yes, honey, if you want to."

The door closed upon the vision of intimate love. Millicent saw Lena walking sedately with the governess of no charm and encyclopaedic information.

"Now we're all right," called Brockton, loudly. "Upon my word, Mrs. Dinsmore, I think you were asleep! Miss Harned, you can't be as entertaining as I thought if your cousin falls asleep with you."

"But think how soothing I must be; that's even better than to be entertaining."

"By ginger! I never found that out—that you were soothing, I mean." It was evident that Mr. Brockton intended a compliment. Anna Dinsmore saw the annoyed red whip out upon Millicent's cheeks. She interposed a few ready, irrelevant questions before the tide of Brockton's flattery.

They made their swift way through the hills, sometimes overlooking the winding course of the river, sometimes skirting the great estates of the region, again whizzing noisily through an old village. Anna and Brockton sustained the weight of conversation. Millicent smiled in vague sympathy with their laughter and Joined at random in the talk. Obstinately her mind had stayed behind her—with the men of Warren, with the round-faced child, and the woman to whose life love and not art gave all its beauty.

They approached one of the larger old towns of the country—a place with a bustling main street and elm-shaded thoroughfares branching from it. Here were ample, well-kept lawns and houses of prosperous dignity. It seemed charming to Millicent with its air of unhurried activity or undrowsy repose.

"What is this, Anna?" she asked.

Anna told her.

"Riverfield?" Millicent repeated the name, but in a strange voice. Anna stared a little.

"Yes. Why? Do you know any one here?"

"No." The word trickled slowly, unwillingly, from Millicent.

"Lovely town, and there are some good places outside," said Anna. "The Ostranders have one, and Jimson, the artist. But the native city, or whatever you call it, is adorable. It has that air of rewarded virtue which makes one ashamed of one's life—"

"I wish"—Millicent still spoke remotely, as if out of a sleep—"I wish, Mr. Brockton, that we might find a little library and museum they have here."

"Why, of course!"

"Are you going to compare it with the Vatican, Millicent?" asked Anna, flippantly. Millicent turned a distant, starry gaze upon her cousin.

"No," she said; and then, in a flash of sympathy and fright, Anna remembered that it had been for some little Berkshire town that Will Hayter had built a library and museum just before his death, six years before—the town from which his family had originally come. Her memory worked rapidly, constructing the story. The blood dyed her face at the thought of her obtuseness. Then she set her lips firmly. She had done her best; if a wanton fate chose to interfere now and make Millicent slave to the phantom of her early, radiant love, she, Anna, could do no more!

"Here we are, I guess," called Brockton. The machine shot into a broad street. A promenade between a double row of elms down its centre gave it a spacious dignity. The modest courthouse stood on one side, as green-bowered as if Justice were a smiling goddess; a few churches broke the stretch of houses. And on the other side the library and museum stood.

"Pretty little building, but plain," commented Brockton, making disparaging note of its graceful severity.

"It's exactly suited to the place; it epitomizes its spirit," said Anna, glibly. "It's austere without being forbidding—perfect Colonial adaptation of the Greek."

Millicent made no architectural observation. Instead she said: "If you don't mind, I should like to go in for a while. You could pick me up later, perhaps on your way back to— Where is it we are lunching?"

Consternation looked out of Anna's eyes, bewilderment out of Brockton's. But Millicent turned to them with such gentle command in her gaze that they could offer no protest.

"Come back in half an hour, if you are ready," she said. Upon Anna, whose baffled look followed her up the flagging between the close-clipt lawns, there came the feeling that she was leaving her cousin alone with the beloved dead.

"Now what—" began Brockton, in full-toned protest,— "what the—"

"That was the last thing Will Hayter did,"—Anna interrupted his question. "And the first, so to speak. It was a fairly important commission. Jessup, the Trya Drop liniment man, came from Riverfield—he has a mammoth place outside now. When he began to coin money faster than the mint, he gave lots of things to his birthplace—which has always blushed for him. It's prouder that Whittier once spent Sunday with one of its citizens than that Alonzo Jessup is its son. Well, he gave the library and museum, and the commission went to Will Hayter. The Hayters came from here two or three generations ago. It was just before his death, and Millicent has been abroad almost ever since. So she had never seen it."

Brockton gave a look of speechless chagrin at his hostess, which she answered haughtily:

"My dear Mr. Brockton, after all, I never undertook to be a marriage-broker!" Then she glanced at the chauffeur and forbore.

Meantime Millicent sat in one of the square exhibition-halls. The sweet air, with the scent of hay from the farther country faintly impregnating it, blew through the quiet. No one else shared the room with her. The even light soothed her eyes, the stillness calmed the fluttering apprehension in her breast which had presaged she knew not what fresh anguish of loss. There were pictures on the walls—one or two not despicable originals which Trya Drop Jessup had given, many copies, and a few specimens of Riverfield's native talent. But she saw none of them, any more than one sees the windows and the paintings in a great cathedral in the first fulness of reverence. To her this was a sacred place. That grief had lost its poignancy, that youth and health with cruel insistence had reasserted their sway over her life, did not mean forgetfulness, unfaith.

"Truly, truly,"—she almost breathed the words aloud,—"there has been no other one. That was my love, young as we were. But I must fill up the days—I must fill up the days."

* * * * *

Her eyes were fixed unseeingly upon a great canvas at the other end of the hall. Some Riverfield hand had portrayed a Riverfield imagination's conception of the moment in the life of Christ when, the temptations of Satan withstood, angels came to Him upon the mountain. In the lower distance the kingdoms of the world grew dim beneath the shadow that fell from the vanquished and retreating tempter, and from the opening heavens a dazzling cloud of angels streamed toward the solitary Figure on the height. By and by Millicent's eyes took note of it. She half smiled. There was daring at least!

Then the picture faded, and again the persistent figure of the child which had so filled her imagination came before her. But this time it was toward herself that the rosy face was turned and limpid eyes lifted in unquestioning dependence. She was the mother; she stood on the piazza, and by her side he stood, who had been so dear in himself, so infinitely dearer in the thought of all that should be; toward them the child came; they were enveloped by breathless love for each other and for that being, innocent, trusting, which their love had called into life. So, dimly, she had dreamed in the radiant days of old. Almost she could feel his hand upon her shoulder, hear his voice full of tenderness that expressed itself only in tone, not in word, taking refuge from too great feeling in jest. She closed her eyes against the vision that made her faint with anguish.

Some one entered the room with a brisk little trot; Millicent opened her eyes and turned her head. A small woman, "old maid" from the top of her neat gray head to the toe of her list shoes, came forward. She held a pad and pencil and wore the badge of authority in her manner. At sight of Millicent she paused, blinking behind her glasses. Millicent came slowly out of her trance; recognition dawned upon her. She rose.

"Miss Hayter—Aunt Harriet!" she cried, advancing.

"It is you, then!" chirped the elder lady. "My dear, who could have expected this?"

"Not I, for one!" She held both Miss Hayter's hands. "I had no idea you were here. Surely you haven't given up your beloved Boston school?"

"Oh no. Only in the summer I come here for a month and substitute for the regular curator while she is on her vacation. It"—she struggled against a constitutional distaste for self-revelation—"it seems like a little visit with Will, somehow."

Millicent's throat throbbed with a strangled sob. No one had spoken his name in so long! Her people had had no interest but to banish the memory of him from her heart; this quaint little aunt of his, who had adored him and lived for him, was the first who had spoken of him in—she did not know how many years. She held tight to the old hands, her eyes clung to the withering face. "Say it again," she whispered; "say his name."

"Why, my dear," cried the older woman, "is it still as hard as this? Come, sit down here with me. Of course I knew that you were not one of the changing kind,"—Millicent winced,—"but I'm sorry to think you should suffer now as keenly as you do."

"It is not just that," said Millicent, shamefacedly. "Only, seeing you unexpectedly gave me a pang. And then, being in the place he built—"

The older woman patted her hand soothingly. "I understand," she said. "I've always understood. When—when you didn't write after the very first, I knew it was because you couldn't, not because you forgot. You were really made for each other, you two. I think I never saw two such radiant, happy creatures in the world. Ah, well!" she wiped a sudden dew from her glasses, "waiting's hard, my dear, but it ends,—it ends."

Millicent was hurt by the unbroken faith in her, by the unquestioning belief she could not share. She looked wistfully upon the shining, tearful eyes.

"It is very beautiful to think that," she said, "but, dear Aunt Harriet, you are mistaken about me. I am going to tell you everything. I—I loved your nephew. I shall not love any one else. It happened to come to me in perfectness when I was young—love. But I live, I am well, I am alive to pleasure and pain. How shall I fill up my life but with the things that still matter to me?"

"You think of marrying, you mean?" Aunt Harriet's voice was dry and harsh. "Well—I am sure Will would wish your happiness, and I—it would not be for me to object. Every day it is done, and very often rightly, I suppose; for money, for companionship, for the chance of self-development, women marry without love. I—I could only wish you happiness."

"You—do not understand."

"My dear,"—her voice softened again; something in the pallor and the quivering pain of the girl touched her,—"I do not mean to speak hardly to you. It seems to me like this: when it comes to piecing out a life that has been broken, as yours was—as mine was, my dear, as mine was—there are two ways of doing it. Either you keep your ideal of perfect love, and lead your poor every-day life of odds and ends, like mine, filling your days with the best scraps of pleasure or usefulness you may, or you give up your ideal of perfect love and marry, and have your home and your children and your rounded outward life. There is, maybe, no question of higher or lower. Each one of us does what her nature bids her. I had always thought of you as one who—But it is not for me to judge."

Her voice was gentle, and she did not look at Millicent. Her eyes seemed to pierce the canvas on the opposite wall and the hangings and the stones behind it, and to see a far image of souls in the struggle of choice. The woman beside her sat silent, her thoughts with the idealists—the men who gave up the comfort of their firesides, the gain of their occupations, and followed whither the vision led; the woman whose home was built upon love and who would see only infamy in houses founded otherwise; the poor soul beside her, stronger in courage, more aspiring in thought, than she, with all her delicacies, her refinements of taste. The ideal had led them all—the ideal, as it had once shone for her and for him whose spirit had informed and beautified the spot where she sat and made her choice.

"Aunt Harriet," she said, and her face was like the sudden flashing of stars between torn clouds,—"Aunt Harriet—" She could not utter the decision in words. "May I come to see you—and learn something from you?"

Miss Hayter looked. There was no need to question. No knight ever rose from his accolade with a face more glorified than Millicent's when she silently dedicated herself to the shining company of those who keep unsullied the early vision.

As she passed out of the hall, her eyes fell again upon the painting of the Temptation. She read the black and gilt legend below it—"And Angels Came and Ministered Unto Him." Then she laughed down upon the old-fashioned figure trotting by her side. "And angels came," she said.

Her rapt look frightened Anna when the automobile returned for her. Then the heart of that frivolous woman was stricken for a moment with wistfulness.

"You seem very happy," she faltered, "and—amused, is it? What are you smiling over?"

"I am still thinking of angels. Would you ever have dreamed, Anna, that they sometimes wore list shoes, and sometimes ate bread and jam, and occasionally spoke with granite lips? They do."

Brockton stirred uneasily, foreboding failure. And Anna sighed, mourning two lost visions.

KEEPERS OF A CHARGE

BY GRACE ELLERY CHANNING

The Doctor's brougham stood at the door; the Doctor's liveried servants waited at the foot of the stairs; the Doctor himself in his study was gathering together his paraphernalia for the day, and the Doctor's face was a study.

He was tired; he was cross; he was feeling ill. His nervous hands were unsteady; his movements were by jerks; his face was a knitted tangle of lines. He had rheumatism in both shoulders, and a headache, and a pain in his chest. He had slept but little, and one of his patients had had the happy idea of despatching a messenger for him in the dead hour of the night. The Doctor never went out nights, and she ought to have known this, but her only son was ill and she was persuaded he could not survive a dozen hours together without the Doctor's personal attendance.

It never seemed to occur to any of his patients that his own life was of the smallest consequence in the balance with theirs or that of any member of their families. Occasionally, when his rheumatism was exceptionally severe or his cough racking, this reflection embittered the Doctor. At other times—and this was generally—he accepted with philosophy this integral selfishness of clients as a part of their inevitable constitution. They were a set of people necessarily immersed and absorbed in their own woes, or in that extension of their woes which was still more passionately their own, and even more unmercifully insisted upon in proportion to the decent veneer of altruism it possessed.

Without being strictly a handsome man, the Doctor produced the effect of one. Nothing gives distinction like character, and this he had and to spare. He was not a popular physician, but a famous one; the day was long past when his professional success depended upon anything so personal as appearance or manner. He could afford to be—and he frequently was—as disagreeable as he felt; desperate sufferers could not afford to resent it, and their relatives, in the grim struggle for a precious life, swallowed without a protest the brusqueries and rebuffs of the man who held in, the hollow of his potent hand their jewel of existence.

He had his passionate detractors and his personal devotees, and these last afflicted him far more than the first. Like the priest, the physician cannot escape taking on superhuman proportions in the eyes of those to whom he has rendered back life, their own or a dearer, and the Doctor (having long outlived the time when it flattered him) was often exasperated to the limits of endurance by the blind faith which asked miracles of him as simply as cups of tea. The strain these women—they were mostly women, of course— put upon him was beyond belief, and he got but a mild pleasure out of the reflection that, being in their nature foolish, they could not help it.

It was quite in keeping, therefore, that one of them should have broken up his night's sleep. He knew those attacks of the boy's by heart; there was exactly one chance in one hundred that his presence should be necessary. He had sent a safe remedy, telephoned a severe but soothing message, and mentally prayed now for patience to meet the irrational, angered eyes of maternity, and to administer a reproof equally gentle and deterrent—gentle, for of course the woman's nerves had to be allowed for; she had been nursing this boy for months. The Doctor slipped into his long, fur-trimmed overcoat and reached for his tall hat.

"You may as well send those Symphony tickets to some-body," he said, impatiently, to his wife; "I sha'n't be able to go. Ten to one I shall be late to dinner, and I doubt if I get home to lunch at all."

His wife, who was patiently holding his gloves and cigar-case, looked at him with a sweet maternal anxiety as he tumbled together the papers on the table, but she only said, "Very well." As he turned to take the gloves and cigar-case, she added, quickly, with a second anxious glance:

"Do try to get a few minutes' rest somewhere. Any of our friends will be so glad to give you a cup of tea—or a little music—and it always rests you so."

The Doctor took the things from her hands; he looked abstractedly at his wife, then stooped hurriedly and kissed her.

"Don't worry about me; I shall be all right," he said, as he hastened from the room. It was characteristic of him that he forgot his clinical thermometer, and was never known to have a prescription-pad or pencil.

One servant opened the house door for him, and another the carriage door; the Doctor stepped in quickly, growling out a direction and ignoring the bows of his retainers. He kept his own for the benefit of his clients, he was wont cynically to say. He settled himself in the seat, and before the door was fairly closed had lighted a cigar and unfurled a medical journal.

As the carriage whirled recklessly down the street and around corners, several feminine patients looked longingly after, as if virtue went out from it, and several masculine ones raised their hats, but the Doctor, his eyes glued to the paper, saw none of them.

Perhaps his most restful moments were these spent in his brougham. It was almost his only time for reading; he had found, moreover, that this served to keep his mind fresh from case to case, detaching it from one train of thought and bringing it with new concentration to the next. These brief intervals belonged wholly to himself. His home was never safe from invasion, and little time and less strength remained to him for domestic joys.

Life had not brought to him all that he was conscious might have been within its gift. Professionally, indeed, he had reached great heights, but these only enabled a measure of the territory beyond, and if to his patients he appeared as a species of demigod, to himself he was merely a "lucky" physician—his peculiar luck consisting in that sixth sense which put him so easily into his patients' skins and pierced through obscure maladies to possible sources. How he knew a great many things puzzled them, but puzzled him still more. Simply at certain crises he was aware that mysteries were momentarily revealed to him. Back of that he possessed, of course, the usual outfit of medical knowledge, open to any one, but which had never yet made a great physician since the world with all its aches and pains began. For *that* other things were needed: a coloring of the artistic temperament, a dash of the gambler's, a touch of femininity, as well as the solid stratum of cool common sense at the bottom of all; *these* eked out the modicum of scientific knowledge which is all mankind has yet wrested from secretive nature. The Doctor sometimes described himself as a "good guesser." Surgery might be an exact science; few things in medicine were exact, and what was never exact was the material upon which medicine must work. The great bulk of his fraternity went through their studious, conscientious, hard-working, and not infrequently heroic lives under the contented conviction of having to deal with two principal facts—disease and medicine—both accessible through study. To them the imponderable factor of the patient represented such or such an aggregation of material—muscle, nerve, blood, brawn, bone, and tissue—which might be counted upon to respond to such and such a treatment in such and such a manner, with very slight variation. The Doctor envied them their simplicity of faith. To him, on the contrary, the patient was a factor which could not be counted on, at all—a force about which he knew virtually nothing, acting upon a mechanism about which he knew little more, and capable of interactions, reactions, and counteractions innumerable, reversing and nullifying all past experience at a moment's notice—an *unforeseen* moment always.

He eyed this mystery, accordingly, with respect, lying in wait for hints from it, and frequently reversing in his turn patiently prepared plans of action, with a prompt speed impossible to a less supple mind,—impossible at all, quite often, to any process of conscious thought. To have these intuitions—that was his touch of femininity; to risk largely upon them was the gambler in him; his swift appropriation of the subject's temperament betrayed the artist in his own; while the hard common sense which drew the rein on all these was a legitimate inheritance—both national and personal. So was his manner—not often extremely courteous and quite often extremely rude. In this latter case his adorers called it "abstracted," while his enemies qualified it as "ill-bred." But his voice, ordinarily abrupt and harsh, could pass to exquisite intonations in the sick-room, and there were moments when to anxious watchers therein, the man seemed more than a man.

The affinity between physician and artist is one of the most curious and suggestive. Every one will recall the famous surgeon-etcher, and the distinguished specialist in nerves and novels. The Doctor's artistic passion was for music. Unfortunately, it was not materially portable, like a writing-pad, and there would have been something unseemly in the spectacle of a physician fiddling in his carriage, so he nursed this love in seclusion. His violin was his one indulgence, and when he permitted himself to dream, it was of a life with music in it. Sometimes he wished his wife were musical; more often he congratulated himself that she was not. He was sincerely attached to her, owing—and, what was more significant, realizing that he owed—her much besides the promising twins; most of all, perhaps, that she consented to be his wife on his own terms. But she was distinctly not musical.

The Doctor laid down his paper and took up his mail, and a disagreeable expression came into his face. It was one of the pleasant features of his professional career that his brother physicians occasionally vented their jealousy of him upon one of their joint patients—stabbing him, so to speak, through *their* lungs or heart, wherein he was most vulnerable. Just as he expected! They had deliberately neglected his prescriptions, after calling him a winter-journey north to deliver them, and as deliberately allowed the victim to die according to their treatment rather than permit him to live according to the Doctor's.

The look upon his face was ugly to behold; he flung open the door with unnecessary violence before the carriage had stopped, and his foot was on the pavement before the footman could descend. Then he braced his rheumatic shoulders for the four steep flights of stairs; he could not justly complain of the number, since he himself had sent the patient there to be high and dry and quiet. On the way up he had one of his nameless seizures of intuition, and in the dark upper hall his hand fell sharply away from the knocker and his face set whitely. There had been just one chance in a hundred that his presence was necessary; before the door opened he knew this had been the hundredth chance.

The ghastly woman's face which met him added nothing to that certitude, yet he winced before it in every nerve.

"You have come too late," she articulated only.

"*No!*" thundered the Doctor. He put her aside like a piece of furniture and strode into the darkened room beyond.

It was more than an hour later when he emerged. The woman stood exactly where he had left her. It was another, tall and young, who turned from the window and looked at him with eyes that hurt. But he did not wince this time.

"It's all right!" he said, cheerfully. His voice quite sang with sweetness. He came and stood a moment by the window, breathing hard. His face was gray, but his eyes smiled, and there was something boyish in his aspect. He looked from one woman to the other sunnily.

"Bless me—you ought never to let yourselves go like that! He'll pull through all right."

The younger woman continued to look at him silently, but the elder, with a long quivering sigh, fainted.

"Best thing she could possibly do," said the Doctor, his

fingers on her pulse. "Get her to bed as soon as you can,— and have these prescriptions sent out. I'll come back later. He'll sleep hours now."

He ran down-stairs, consulting his visiting-list as he ran, and jumped into the brougham, calling an address as he pulled the door to with a slam. This time, however, he did not take out his papers, but sat with an unlighted cigar between his lips, gazing intently at nothing.

In the course of the next few hours he looked over an assortment of ailing babies, soothed as many distracted mothers, ordered to a gay watering-place one young girl whom he was obliged to treat for chronic headache—chronic heartache not being professionally recognizable,—administered the pathetically limited alleviations of his art to a failing cancer-patient (she happened to be a rich woman, going with the fortitude of the poor down the road to the great Darkness), and so, looking in on various pneumonias and fevers, broken souls and bruised bodies, by the way, brought up at last at the hospital to see how yesterday's operation was going on. It was going on in so very mixed a manner that he telephoned he should not return to lunch—prophesying long after the event.

It was turning dusk when he started on his second round of visits homeward, stopping on the outskirts to rebandage, in one of the tenements, a child's broken arm. He had not returned his footman's salutation that morning, but had carried in his subconsciousness all day this visit to the footman's child. In one manner or another that inconvenient locality had been compassed in his circuit for the past three weeks. From it he passed to his daily ordeal, another rich patient, a nervous wreck, whose primary ailment—the lack of anything to do—had passed into the advanced stages of an inability to do anything, with its sad Nemesis of melancholia—the registered protest of the dying soul. It was a case which took more out of the Doctor than all his day's practice put together; he always came from it in a misery of doubts.

The dusk was becoming the dark when he set his foot wearily on the carriage step once more, and with his hand on the carriage door paused suddenly. He was sick of sickness, mortally tired of mortality! For the first time in the whole day he hesitated; an odd, irresolute look came into his face; he pulled out his watch, glanced, and changing his first-given address for another, threw himself back on the cushions with closed eyes. He did not open them again until the carriage, rolling through many streets, came to a halt under some quiet trees, before an apartment-house. There were yellow daffodils between white curtains—very white and high up. As he stepped out, the Doctor glanced involuntarily towards them, and a half-breath of relief escaped him, instantly quenched in a nervous frown and jump as his arm was seized by a firm gloved hand.

"Doctor,—this is really *providential!* You are the very person I wished to see!"

It was the younger of two heavily upholstered and matronly ladies who spoke, in a voice of many underscorings. The Doctor, who had removed his hat with a purely mechanical motion, knew himself a prey, identified his captor, and eyed her with restrained bitterness.

"Doctor,—it is about my Elsie;—she hasn't a particle of color, and she complains of feeling languid all the time—"

"No wonder!—What do you expect?"—it was the Doctor's harshest tone. "She is loaded up with flesh,—she doesn't exercise,—you stuff her. Send her out with her hoop,—make her drink water,—stop stuffing her. What she, wants is thinning out."

"*Elsie!*—Why, Doctor, the child eats *nothing,*—I have to tempt her all the time;—and when she goes out she complains of feeling tired."

"Let her complain,—and let her get tired;—it will do her good. Don't feed her in betweentimes,—and when you do feed her, give her meat—something that will make red blood,—not slops, nor sweets, nor dough. There's nothing in the world the matter with her." He lifted his hat and strode on up the stairs.

Maternity, grieved and outraged, stared after him, speechless, then turned for sympathy in the nearest feminine eye.

"Really, dear,—I think that was almost *vulgar,*—as well as unkind," murmured the other mother at her side.

"*Vulgar! Unkind!* Well, it is the last time he will have the opportunity to insult me! The idea! *Elsie!*—But it's not the first time I have thought of changing physicians!" (This was true,—but she never did; the solid Elsie was her only one.) "And such desperate haste;—he must have a *most critical* case!" She cast an indignant glance at the building, as if to make it an accessory to the fact, and turning a kindling and interrogative glance upon her companion, encountered one of profound and scintillating significance. For a moment they contemplated their discovery breathlessly in each other's eyes.

"Did you ever!" exclaimed number one at last. "Oh, of course I had heard things,—but I will do myself the justice to say I *never* believed a word of it before! *This,* of course, makes it plain enough;—this explains *all!*"

The two—good women, but wounded withal—coruscated subtle knowledge all down the street.

Meantime the Doctor climbed the stairs. He was perfectly conscious that he had been, in fact, both unkind and rude, even though his mood did not incline him to take measure of the extent of his delinquency. He knew equally that he should presently have to write a note of apology—and that it would not do an atom of good, *Tant pis*. He rang at the door of the daffodil-room, and it was opened by the tall girl whose eyes had hurt him that morning. They did not hurt him now, but enveloped him with a keen and soft regard that left no question unanswered. In another moment she had put out a firm hand and drawn him over the threshold in its clasp.

"Don't speak,—don't try to say a word! There!" She had taken from him his hat and gloves and pushed forward a low chair in front of the fire, all in one capable movement. "What is it? Tea? Coffee? A glass of wine?"

"*Music!*" answered the Doctor, raising two haggard eyes, with the exhausted air of an animal taking shelter.

The girl turned away her own and walked towards the piano, stopping on the way, however, to push forward a little table set forth with a steaming tea-urn and cups, matches and a tray, and to lift to its farther edge a bowl of heavy-scented violets. Her every motion was full of ministry, as devoid of fuss.

The room was low, broad, and large, and full of books, flowers, low seats, and leaping firelight. A grand-piano, piled with music, dominated the whole. The girl seated herself before it and began to play, with the beautiful, powerful touch of control. After the first bars, the Doctor's head sank back upon the cushions of the chair and the

Doctor's hand stole mechanically to the matches. He smoked and she played—quiet, large music, tranquilly filling the room: Bach fugues, German Lieder, fragments of weird northern harmonies, fragments of Beethoven and Schubert, the Largo of Handel,—and all the time she played she looked at the man who lay back in the chair, half turned from her, the cigar drooping from his fingers. There was no sound in the room but the music and light leaping of little flames in the fireplace,—no motion but theirs and the pulsing fingers on the keys. The girl played on and on, till the fire began to die, and with a sudden sigh the Doctor held up his hand. Then she rose at once, and going forward, stood as simply at the side of the fireplace opposite him. She was not beautiful, but, oh, she was beautiful with health and calm vigor.

The Doctor let his eyes rest on her.

"If you knew," he said, with a little, half-apologetic laugh.

In her turn she held up one of her long hands.

"But I do;—you forget I was there all the morning. And you pulled him through. As for the rest—" She stooped suddenly and began to pile together the logs; the Doctor watched her, noting with a trained and sensitive eye the muscular ease and grace of the supple arms and shoulders—like music. "Of course"—she spoke lightly—"they will kill you some day, among them; but—it's worth while, isn't it?—and there isn't much else that is, is there?" Still kneeling, she turned and looked straight up at him. "Do you know what it was like this morning—before you came?"

The Doctor shook his head.

She hesitated a moment, smiling a little. "'Lord, *if Thou hadst been here*, our brother had not died!'" she quoted.

The Doctor got up quickly from his chair. He knocked the ash from his cigar and laid it down on the tray. "Well," he said, lightly, "I must be off." He squared his shoulders and held out his hand; its grip upon her own trembled very slightly, but he smiled sunnily. "I'll come back for some more music some day."

"Do," the girl said. She had risen and was smiling too.

The Doctor looked about the room wistfully. "Jolly place,—I don't get up very often, do I?"

"Not very."

They smiled at each other again, then the girl, turning abruptly away, walked to the window and came back with a double handful of yellow flowers.

"Will you carry these to your wife? They are the first of the year."

She held the door open for him, and from the little landing watched him down the stairs. At their turn he glanced up for a moment, holding his hat raised silently. She waved him a mute acknowledgment, then going into the room again, closed the door.

The firelight still leaped languidly on the hearth, and on the half-smoked cigar and pile of ashes in the tray. The girl stood a moment looking at these things and the chair, then walked quietly to the piano and sat down before it. But she did not play again.

Meantime the Doctor, an erect and urgent presence in the dusk, had driven through dim streets and climbed again the four flights of the morning, to find the hush of heaven fallen on the house.

"I knew *you* could save him!" said the pale mother only, lifting blind eyes of worship from the couch.

The Doctor laughed, poured her out with his own hands a sleeping-draught, and sat patiently beside her till she slept, then stole away, leaving injunctions with the nurse, established in his absence, to telephone if there came a crisis—"even," after a moment's hesitation, "in the night."

"Home!"—he gave the order briefly. There were black circles beneath his eyes, making him look thinner than when he left the house that morning; he had no distinct reminiscence of lunch, and he was very tired; but his shoulders no longer ached, his headache was gone, and his hands were perfectly steady.

Odd bits of music hummed perversely through his head, mixing themselves up with all things and rippling the air about him into their own large waves, bearing now and then upon them, like the insistent iteration of an oratorio chorus, fantastic fragments—"If Thou hadst been here!—If Thou hadst been here!" His fingers ached towards the responsive strings, and pulling out his watch, he made a hasty calculation. There should be good fifteen minutes, he decided—toilet allowed for—and he hurried the coachman again and leaned forward, looking with bright, eager eyes into the night, and humming to himself.

One liveried servant opened the house door, another the carriage door, and a third relieved him of his hat and coat. Out of the warmth and brightness his wife advanced to meet him, a child in either hand, their long curls brushed and tied with bright ribbons. Her face was filled with tender solicitude.

"You must be worn out;—what a long day you have made! Would you like the dinner sent in at once, or would you rather wait? Children, don't hang so on papa; he must be dreadfully tired. Oh, and there's a man been waiting over an hour; he simply *wouldn't go*; but you'll let him come back to-morrow?—you won't try to see any one else tonight?"

The Doctor hesitated a moment, letting all the warmth and brightness sink into him, while his hands played with the soft hair of his little son and daughter. He smiled at his wife, a bright, tired smile.

"Robin," he said, "run down to the carriage; there are some posies there for mamma—from Miss Graham, Louise,—you see I did get a moment's rest."

"Yes," said his wife. She continued to gaze compassionately at the tired man. After a moment she repeated gently, "And the dinner, dear—?"

"No,—don't wait for me; I'll not be long. Have it brought in at once, and—send the man into the office, please."

He stooped and kissed the children, and turning away, went into his office and closed the door behind him.

A WORKING BASIS

BY ABBY MEGUIRE ROACH

Why she married him her friends wondered at the time. Those she made later wondered more. Before long she caught herself wondering. Yes, she had seen it beforehand, more or less. But she had seen other things as well: he had developed unevenly, unexpectedly, if logically. There had been common tastes—which grew obsolete or secondary. As the momentum of what she believed and hoped of him ran down with them both, he crystallized into the man he was, and no doubt virtually had always been.

It was bad enough to have to ask for money, but to have it counted out to you, to be questioned about it like a child, was worse.

"I don't understand," she said in the first months of their marriage. "Are you afraid I won't be judicious, responsible? Mightn't you try before judging?"

"Judicious? Responsible?" He pinched her cheek. (Judith was five feet nine and sweetly sober of mien.) "There are no feminines or diminutives of those words, my dear."

She stepped back. "But with more freedom I could manage

better, Sam."

"Manage?"—jocularly. "That *is* your long suit, isn't it? You feel equal to managing all of us? Could even give me pointers on the business, eh?"

"Why not?" she asked, quietly.

Sam, feet apart, hands in pockets, looked her over with the smile one has for a dignified kitten. "I won't trouble you, my dear. I manage this family." With his pleasantries a lower note struck—and jangled.

"But that isn't the point. I want—"

"Really? You always do. Don't bother to tell me what. If you got this you'd be wanting something else, so what's the use of the expense merely to change the object?" He chuckled at her baffled silence.

"I can't answer when you're like that. But—but, Sam! It isn't fair!" Still she supposed that relevant.

However, money was not the chief thing. He could manage. Let it go.

Having properly impressed her, nothing made Sam feel larger than to bring her a set of pearl-handled knives,—when she had wanted a dollar for kitchen tins. His extravagances were not always generosities. Once, after she had turned her winter-before-last suit and patched new seats into the boy's flannel drawers, because "times were hard," he bought a brace of blooded hunting-dogs.

Next day she opened an account at a department store.

With the promptness of the first of the month and the sureness of death, the bill came. Sam had expressed himself unchecked before she turned in the doorway. "If you will go over it," she said, with all her rehearsal unable, after all, to imitate his nonchalance, "you will find nothing unnecessary. I think there is nothing there for the dogs."

But her cannon-ball affected him no more than a leaf an elephant; he did not know he was hit. It was always so.

In his cool way, however, Sam had all the cumulative jealousy of the primitive male for his long primacy. Some weeks later, when Judith ordered an overcoat for Sam junior sent home on approval, she found the store had been instructed to give her no credit.

She got out, with burning face and heart, without the article. Her first impulse was to shrink from a blow.

But at table that night she recounted her experience: "The very courteous gentleman who informed me of your predicament happened to be a cousin of Mr. Banks, of Head and Banks. (They supply your grain, I believe?) Mrs. Howe (isn't it R. E. Howe who is president of the Newcomb Club?) was at my elbow. The salesgirl has Sam junior's Sunday-school class. Doubtless it will interest them all to know you are in such straits you can't clothe your children."

Ah? She had touched his vulnerable point? Instantly she was swept by compunction, by impulses to make amends, to him, to their love. Their love! That delicate wild thing she kept in a warm, moist, sheltered place, and forbore to look at for yellowing leaves.

Like the battle of Blenheim, it was a famous victory, but what good came of it at last? The overcoat came home, to be sure, with cap and shoes besides. But she was too gallant to press her advantage. Besides, she still looked for him to take a hint.

He did, after his own fashion. "You ought to see Judith here," he laughed to a caller, "practising her kindergarten methods on me." His imperturbability was at once a boast and a slight.

"He doesn't mean it," she apologized, later, protecting herself by defending him. "You know how men are; the best of them a bit stupid about some things. They don't mean to hurt you. You know it, but you can't help crying."

"Oh, I understand!" (That any one should sympathize with her! It was not so much her vanity that suffered as her precious regard for him, her pride in their marriage.) "Nobody minds little things like that against such devotion and constancy. Why, he talks of you all the time, Judith; of your style, your housekeeping. You are his pet boast. He says you can do more with less than anybody he ever saw." And then Judith laughed.

They were all articles of the creed she herself repeated—and doubted more and more. Faithful enough. He never came or went without the customary kiss. When he had typhoid fever, no one might be near him but her, until her exhaustion could no longer be concealed, when he fretted about her—until he fretted himself back into high temperature and had a relapse.

So, run down as she was, she hid it, kept up, went on alone, adding to the score of her inevitable day of reckoning, after the old heroic-criminal woman-way.

She had begun with ideas of their saving together for a purpose; but, not allowed to plan, she must use every opportunity to provide against future stricture; besides, Sam's arbitrary and unregulated spending made her poor little economies both futile and unfair.

"I know nothing about your business. How can I tell if I spend too much?"

"Make your mind easy; I'll keep you posted," he laughed. *He* was not bothering about dangerous ground.

"Doubtless,"—dryly. "But if I spend too little?"

"Not you."

He did mean it! He didn't care! The half-truth fanned the slow fire growing within her into sudden flame. Judith turned, stammering over the dammed rush of replies.

"My dear, my dear!" he deprecated, amused. "How easily you lose your temper lately, every time there is a discussion of expenses! Why excite yourself?" Why, indeed? Anger put her at a disadvantage, and making her half wrong, half made him right. "I don't say I particularly blame you, but you see for yourself you don't keep your balance, and it's mistaken kindness to tempt any woman's natural feminine weakness for luxury and display."

The retorts were so obvious they were hopeless. She stood looking at him.

His eyebrows lifted; he shrugged his shoulders, went out, and forgot.

Why any of it, indeed? There was no bridge of speech between alien minds. Their life was a continual game of cross-questions and silly answers. Their natures were antipodal; he had the faults that annoyed her most; his virtues were those least compensating.

Was her dream of influencing the children a superstition too, then?

The children! They slipped the house whenever possible; avoided their father with an almost physical effect of dodging an expected blow; when with him, watched his mood to forestall with hasty attention or divert with strained wit, with timorous hilarity when he proved complaisant. The possibilities for harm to them were numberless. She and Sam were losing the children, and the children were losing everything.

For years they had been a physical and mental outlet for her nature. That love had no question of reciprocity or merit. She had always been willing for them. Only it seemed to her all the rest of love should come first. It occurred to her ironically how happy her marriage would have been without her husband.

What was his love worth? It was only taxation—taxation without representation. Had either of them any real love left?

Suddenly she stood on the brink of black emptiness. To live without love; her whole nature, every life-habit, changed! *Oh, no, no, no!* So the cold water sets the suicide struggling for shore.

Dear, dear! This would not do. Her nerves were getting the best of her; she was losing her own dignity and sweetness— was on the verge of a breakdown.

But to say so would be to invoke doctors, pointless questions, futile drugs, and a period of acute affection from

Sam—affection that took the form chiefly of expecting it of her.

At times Judith thought of death as an escape, but she thought of no other as being any more in her own hands; like so many people, she quoted the Episcopal marriage-service as equal authority with the Bible. She was too live to droop and break as some do. She had not made herself the one armor that would have been effective—her own shell. Friction that does not callous, forms a sore. Her love, her utmost self, ached like an exposed nerve. She had not dreamed one's whole being could be so alive to suffering. She must be alone, to get a hand on herself and things again.

At table one night she wanted them all to know she was going away, for several months perhaps, leaving her cousin Anne in charge. It was all arranged.

The amazing innovation surprised Sam into speechlessness.

Judith had had few vacations. There had always been the babies, of course. And Sam's consent had always been so hard to get. His first impulse about everything was to refuse, contradict, begrudge. Then certainly he mustn't be too easily convinced. After that he always moped through her preparations; counted and recounted the cost, and at the last perhaps gave her a handsome new bag when her old one was particularly convenient, and he had supplied only half she had asked for clothes; would hardly tell her good-by for desolate devotion; tracked her with letters full of loneliness, ailments, discomforts. When she had cut short her plans and hurried back, a bit quiet and unresponsive perhaps, "How truly gracious your unselfishness is, my dear!" he observed. "If it comes so hard to show me a little consideration, you would really better keep doing your own way."

"I never do my own way."

"No? Whose then? I fail to recognize the brand."

"That's the trouble. I might as well stop trying."

Now, she could not delay for, nor endure, the conventional comedy.

Since he asked her no questions, she hastened to explain: "I want to rest absolutely. Not even to write letters. You need not bother to, either. Anne will let me know if I am needed. And if I need anything, you will be sure to hear."

"Oh, sure." Sam was recovering.

But he couldn't think she would really go, in that way at least. He thought he knew one good reason why not. Yet, vaguely on guard against her capacity for surprise, he did not risk the satire of asking her plans. To the last Judith hoped he would shame her a little by offering the money; and against his utter disregard her indignation rose slowly, steadily, deepening, widening, drowning out every other feeling for him.

When, after their final breakfast, he kissed her good-by as for the morning only, she took her jewelry and silver, mementos of his self-indulgence in generosity, and pawned them, mailing him the tickets from the station where she piloted herself alone.

She spent a month (in her rest-cure!), writing and destroying letters to him. There was no alternation of moods now. Nor was she seeking a solution of the problem; there was only one.

At last a letter seemed to do: "It cannot hurt you to read, as much as me to write. But it must come. I can see now it has always been coming. Things cannot go on as they are. We are unable to improve them together. I will cast no blame. Perhaps some other woman would have called out a different side of you, or would have minded things less. It is enough that we do not belong together, because we are we and cannot change. We are not only ruining each other's happiness—that is already irrevocable,—we are ruining each other, and the children, and their futures. It is a question of the least wrong. And I am not coming back.

"I want the children, all of them. But if you insist, you take Sam junior and I the girls—and the baby, of course, at least for the present. And you shall provide for us proportionately. There is no use pretending independence; I have given my strength and all the accomplishments I had to you and them. And there is no sense in the mock-heroics that I don't want your money. It isn't your money; it's ours, everything we have. I have borne your children, and saved and kept house and served and nursed for you and them. If you want to divide equally now, I will take that as my share forever. But we can't escape the fact that we have been married and have the children."

She could get an answer in two days.

But it did not come in two days, nor two weeks, nor three; while she burned herself out waiting.

Moreover, her funds were running low. She had waves of the nausea of defeat, fevers of the desperation of the last stand.

Then it occurred to her. Her armor had always been defensive. She had never stooped to neutralize his alkali with acid. But there was one weapon of offence she occasionally used. She wrote: "I am drawing on you to-day through your First National for a hundred and fifty. You will honor it, I think. And if I do not hear from you in a day or two I shall have Judge Harwood call on you as my attorney."

The answer came promptly enough:—"My dear child, I couldn't make out what had struck you, so I hoped you would just feel better after blowing off steam and would get over your fit of nerves. Besides, I have nothing to say except to quote yourself: 'We can't escape the fact that we are married and have the children.' I know you too well to be afraid of your throwing off all obligations like that. It is impossible to fancy you airing our privacies." Bait? or a goad? Oh yes, he counted on her "womanly qualities"—but with no idea of masculine emulation! "If you need advice, think what either of our mothers would say." Her mother! Judith could hear her, "His doing wrong cannot make it right for you to," with logic so unanswerable one forgot to question its relevance. And his! Judith held her partly accountable; some women absolutely fostered tyranny. Their mothers, poor things! Occasionally their fathers were different, but so occasionally that now the times were. "This sudden mood strikes me as very remarkable. 'After all I have done—twelve years of grind to keep you from the brunt of the world; and now...! My dear child, do you realize that there are husbands with violent tempers, husbands who drink and gamble and worse?

"I honored your draft. Do not try it again. And I advise you to use it to come home. We will have Dr. Hunter give you a tonic, and you will find you have fewer morbid fancies occupied with your duties. I shall look for you the end of the week." Surely Sam was moved quite out of himself, that he had no lashes of laughter for her. But the next was more in character: "Bridget threatens to leave. She does not work well under Anne. The children are not manageable under her, either. Little Judith is sallow and fretful. I suspect Anne gives her sweets between meals. I saw a moth flying in my closet to-day...."

Judith pushed the letter away, fidgeted, yet smiled. How well they knew each other. And they used it only to sting and bully! Surely it could be put to better purpose. Had she tried *everything*? Had Sam fully understood? Sometimes she thought her early excuses had hurt too much for her to admit their truth: much of his unkindness was not intentional, only stupid; slow sympathy, dull sensibility; he did not suffer, nor comprehend, like a savage or a child. If the possibility of separation was new to her, would not he never have thought of it at all? But now, might he not see? Was not his unwonted self-defence itself admission of new enlightenment and approachability?

She sat long in the increasing dusk. Exhausted with struggle, loneliness was on her, crying need of the children, return to the consideration of many things. Admitting that at times it was right to break everything, wrong not to, it was at least the last resort. Love, of course, was over irrevocably; but were there not some things worth saving? Could not she and Sam find some working basis?

What had made their being together most intolerable to her was their persistence in the religion of a vanished god in whose empty ceremonies alone they could now take part together. Of the sacred image nothing was left but the feet of clay. Freed of that desecration, she could cure or endure everything else; her obligations, moreover, would hardly conflict at all.

Looking back at the pressures of nature, society, events, Sam's persistence, she wondered at times if, from the beginning, she had been any more responsible for her marriage than for the color of her hair. There were many such explanations for Sam, too. Not that they made her like him any better, feel him any more akin. But it was true that between the fatalities of heredity and environment that "slight particular difference" that makes the self had but short tether for action and reaction. Oh, she could be generous enough to him if he did not have to be part of herself!

She got up, lit the gas, shutting out the stars, and wrote: "I am coming back to make one more and one last effort. *Won't you*?" If he would only try!

Sam met her with the magnanimity of forgiveness, the consciousness of kind forgetting. Her redeemed valuables were all in place. Everything should be the same, in spite of—And she put the back of her hand against his lips!

When he dressed for dinner the salvage of the three balls, the spoils of war, were piled in his bureau drawer.

Still he hoped better for the roses by her plate. She had the maid carry them out, explaining in her absence, "No gifts, please, Sam. Substitutes will not do any longer."

Sam played with his fork, smiling, with lips only. How shockingly she showed suffering. Separation had made her appearance unfamiliar; he thought the change all recent. He took pains to compliment the immediate improvement in the pastry, to give her the servants' money unreminded as soon as they were alone.

How characteristic! Judith thought, wearily, letting the bills lie where he laid them.

"That's one of the things for us to settle, Sam," she said, in her new freedom and self-respect discarding the familiar

Various Authors

little diplomacies by which she was used to soothe, prepare, manage, the lord of the hearth. "I am not going to ask for money in the future, nor depend on what you happen to give." The manner was a simple statement of fact. "You must make me an allowance through your bookkeeper."

Sam was lounging through his cigar. "So that's it? Still?" He smiled confidentially at the smoke, puffing it from his lower lip. "As accurately as I can recollect, my dear, I have told you seven thousand and three times that I am not on a salary, and don't know from month to month what I will make."

How unchanged everything was! Her determination stiffened. "But you know what you have made. Base it on the year before. Or have a written statement mailed me every month, and file my signature at the bank."

Not quite unchanged; for Sam took the cigar from his mouth and turned slowly to look at her. If he had taken her return for capitulation and had met it according to his code, things were not fitting in. "Really, my dear! Really! What next? Evidently I have never done you justice; you have positive genius in the game—of monopoly; first thing, *I'll* be begging from *you*."

Well, why not, as fairly? and why should he think better of her than of himself? But it was too old to go over again. For a breath she waited to see her further way. She had not planned this as the issue, but the moment was obviously crucial, and offered what, in international politics already awry, would constitute a good technical opportunity. If her mirage of regeneration, her hope of an understanding, perhaps even her love, had flung up any last afterglow in this home-coming, it was over now. Indeed, now it seemed an old grief, the present but confirmation concerning a lover ten years lost at sea. She saw the whole man now clearly, the balance of her accusations and excuses; he had neither the modern spirit of equality, nor the medieval quixotism of honor and chivalry; appeal merely stirred the elemental tyranny of strength and masculinity, held as a "divine right"; weakness tempted an instinctive cruelty, half unconscious, half defiant.

It was Sam who spoke first, abruptly, not laughing. Sam who was never angry, was angry now. "I never have understood you in some ways. How a woman like you can forever bring money between us! How you got tainted with this modern female anarchy! You seem to forget that *I* made the money, it is *mine*. There is bound to be discussion; I never knew any one so determined to have everything his own way. All the same," the defence rested its case, "it takes two to quarrel, and I won't."

No, his defence was only admission of conscious weakness. He was afraid—of the solution she had discarded. She did not go back to it now. But now she saw the way, the only way, to accomplish reconstruction.

Judith looked at him steadily. Her voice was deadly quiet. "I am sure I have made myself quite plain. We will never discuss this again. You can let me know in the morning which arrangement you choose."

They faced each other with level eyes.

And Sam's shifted.

He never had real nerve, she realized; they didn't—that kind. How had she managed to love him so long?

Late that night he knocked at her door with a formal proposition: Would that do?—dumbly. She changed a point or two: *That* would do, and signified good night. Sam, looking at her face, turned away from it, hesitated, turned back, broke. Fear increased his admiration, and, to do him justice, the fear was not wholly for conventions and comforts; the man had certain broad moralities and loyalties. A reflex muscular action had set in to regain what he had lost. "Judith! Judith!" he begged.

Her raised hand stopped him. "You are too late, Sam."

"My dear, you mustn't get the idea that I don't love you still."

"Love has nothing to do with it any more. Besides, it is never any use to talk of love without justice."

He went out, dazed and aggrieved. He had always thought they got along as well as most people. *He* had not been cherishing grudges.

Womanlike, having met the emergency gallantly, after it was all over Judith collapsed. The day of reckoning for which she had so long been running up an account was on her. But the growing assurance rallied her, that her going away and her coming back were equally means to her success in failure.

The reality of their marriage could not have been saved. But they had the children; and to the children was restored much of what their father had largely spoiled in the first place, and she nearly forfeited in the second. For the fact was that Sam did better; the despot is always a moral coward, and always something of the slave to a master. Moreover, her growing invulnerability to hurt through him set, in large measure, the attitude of the household; everybody was more comfortable. She discounted his opinions and complaints; but, in considering the welfare of the greatest number, she sacrificed as little as possible his individual comforts. His interests she studied. And for the rest, she let him go his way and went hers.

Life is a perfect equation: if something is added or subtracted, something is subtracted or added, so long as there *is* life. Judith got her poise again in time, as strong natures do after any death; with some fibres weakened past mending, gray, but calm. If his side of her nature was stunted, she seemed to blossom all the more richly in other ways. She loved her children in proportion as she had suffered and worked for them. After her domestic years, like so many women, she took fresh start, physically and mentally. Her executive ability found public outlet. She could admit friends again. Freedom from the corrosion of antagonism was happiness. Without the struggle to keep that love which must ask so much of its object, she could give Sam more of that altruism which asks nothing.

THE GLASS DOOR

BY MARY TRACY EARLE

Charlotte and Emory Blake lived at the old Blake place, on the little plateau at the foot of the Colton hill, in a vine-covered stone cottage. The place had belonged to old George Blake. When it came into Emory's hands he sold it to Uncle Billy Kerr, and used the money for a course in a school of pharmacy. Later, Charlotte, who was then Charlotte Hastings, bought it, and, after her marriage, finished paying for it out of its own products, while her husband talked politics or played chess in his drug-store. It was said that when Blake was doing either of these things he was as likely as not to keep a customer standing a half-hour before waiting on him,—and this not so much out of interest in his discussion or his game as from complete lack of interest in the business of selling drugs.

North Pass correctly interpreted this general nonchalance of Blake's as a sign that he was an unwilling partner in the matrimonial venture he had undertaken. Indeed, it was known that the engagement had hung fire for years through no fault of Charlotte's, and everybody had noticed that such mildly loverlike enthusiasm for her society as Blake had shown before he went to the school of pharmacy had disappeared from his manner when he returned. Charlotte had told people that they should marry as soon as he came home, yet the wedding did not come off for two years. During this time it was noticed that although she held her head high and was fertile in good reasons for the delay, her girlish look left her, her features sharpened, and her speech developed an acid reaction; it was at this time, too, that she bargained with Uncle Billy Kerr for the old Blake place, and also borrowed money from the old man to put up a new house. When people saw the house going up it was generally supposed that she was preparing either to rent it or to live in it as an old maid; but when it was completed, to the surprise of every one, Charlotte and Blake were married and moved in.

The morning after the wedding Blake was in his drug-store playing chess as languidly as ever, but Charlotte spent her whole day planting a vegetable-garden, in a mood of unreckoning exaltation such as rarely comes to a woman of her nature, and never comes to her but once. She had felt no such blissful security when Blake and she were first engaged. Blake was weak. She had felt it intensely even when her infatuation for him was too fresh to permit her to reason, and a weak man while unmarried is peculiarly liable to changes of affection. But, on the other hand, a weak man once safely married is completely in the power of his wife; during the last two years of their engagement certain illusions regarding herself and Blake had fallen from her eyes; she had stated both those facts plainly to herself, and they had helped her to decide upon a course of action. There had been moments when she had despised herself for using her stronger will to coerce Blake into the fulfilment of his engagement, but on the morning after the wedding these moments were forgotten, and, as she hoed and raked and planted in the brisk air and the bright spring sunshine, her whole existence seemed uplifted by the knowledge that she and Blake at last belonged unquestionably to each other; that every output of her strength was for their common comfort, and would continue to be as long as they both should live.

As the first year of married life goes, Charlotte's first year was fairly successful. She knew Blake's faults already, and had made up her mind to them, and if there was a frank indifference in his quiet languor, she had made up her mind to that, too. He was never unkind, and there were times when some fresh evidence of her devotion to him would touch him into an appreciation that was almost responsive. And there were other times when she would find him looking at her with an expression which any other observer might have classed as pity, but which she counted as tenderness. On the whole, it seemed to her that time was bringing them together, as she had counted that it would, and with this hope her face lost its sharp outlines.

Her first heavy chagrin was at the time of her baby's birth. When Blake came into the room to inquire for her, and she turned down the bed-cover to show him the little bundle at her side, a look of pain and aversion flashed across his face, and he moved away, begging her not to show the baby to him until it was older. On another day she tried to make him select a name for it, and he refused.

"Call it anything you please," he said at first, but she would not let him go at that.

"I've been thinking," she suggested, with a hesitation that was foreign to her,—"I've been thinking of calling her for your mother—Dorcas."

They were alone in the room, and he was sitting by her bed, but looking away from her into the corner of the room, while she looked anxiously at him. At her words he started, flashing a keen glance at her. "Why should we name her that?" he asked.

There was something so sharply disturbed in his manner, and his distaste for the idea was so evident, that Charlotte flushed in extreme embarrassment.

"I thought you might like to," she explained.

"Well, I wouldn't,—I—I don't think the name's pretty in itself," he declared; adding, with a great effort to speak naturally, "I'd rather name her for you."

Charlotte's lips came together so closely that all the unpleasant lines showed around them. "I certainly shall not name her for myself," she said. "You must think of some other name."

Blake got to his feet. "That's the only one I can think of," he said. "If you don't like it, you can take some other. It's your affair, not mine."

Charlotte's eyes flashed and then filled with tears, for she was very weak. "If I were asking you to father some other man's child, you couldn't act more as if you despised me," she sobbed.

He turned as he was leaving the room and gave her a long look full of exasperation, repugnance, and despair. "You are quite mistaken," he said. "I don't despise you. I despise myself."

For half an hour Charlotte sobbed, her hands clenched at her sides, her tears flowing unchecked; then, quite suddenly, she was calm, and, drying her disfigured face, she began to take account of stock. All that she had before, she reasoned, she still had. The gains of a year might seem to be lost in the outbreak of a moment, yet they still existed as a solid foundation to build upon. There would be constraint at first, but the effort of daily patience would overcome it in time; moreover, there was the baby. Blake might refuse to look at her now, but as she grew and acquired the irresistible graces of a healthy babyhood he would be obliged to see and to yield to her. A man of his nature could not live in the house with a child and not love it. She touched the small form at her side, as if to assure herself that this ally which she had so suffered for had not deserted her. Yes, she had more hope now than ever before, she told herself, and her eyes shone with a passionate tenderness, though her lips were set in a hard line. Suddenly the line broke into a smile.

"I'll name her Hope," she said.

When Hope was two months old she began her mission, and when she had reached six months Blake was vying with Charlotte in his devotion to her. He even plucked up a little interest in his business; sometimes he talked over his place with his wife, and the words which had passed between them over the naming of the child, though unforgotten, seemed so far in the past that Charlotte's courage strengthened with each day. The sense of security which had marked the first months of her married life did not return, but she could feel herself making a strong fight against fate to hold what she had, and, if she were never entirely certain of the issue, at least she fought with the obstinacy which has no knowledge of yielding. Sometimes even her love for Blake seemed to lose itself in this obstinacy, and her tenderness towards her child seemed the only womanly sentiment left in her; but more often her love for her husband mounted high and unmixed above the other feelings as the tremendous, inexplicable passion of her life.

Hope's attainment of six months was marked by an unusual display of energy on the part of Blake. The first cold weather of autumn had come, and when the house doors were closed,

Charlotte was surprised to hear her husband declare that the sitting-room, where the baby would spend most of her time in winter, was poorly lighted, and needed to have a glass door substituted for the wooden one which opened on to the front porch. Still more to her surprise, the door was delivered from an adjoining town the next day, and on the following morning Blake rose earlier than usual and hung it before going down to his store. It was the first time he had lifted his hand towards the improvement of Charlotte's house.

He whistled boyishly while he measured and fitted in the hinges, and when it came to holding the door while the hinges were screwed in place, he called to Charlotte. She came, with lips as usual closed very tight, but with cheeks flushed very pink, and when the work was finished she was so atremble that she had to sit down for a moment before she could put breakfast on the table.

To give a reason for the delay, she kept looking at the door. "The room, is perfect now," she said.

Blake swung the new acquisition back and forth, and latched it once or twice to make sure that it was perfectly adjusted. When he was satisfied he glanced at his wife.

"It will give our baby the sunlight," he said, and their eyes met for a moment.

All that day, whenever Charlotte could bring her work into the sitting-room, she sat facing the glass door. She was not exactly happy; she was too strangely excited for happiness; but she was keenly awakened and alert. Every nerve in her seemed keyed up to its ultimate tension, and if the shadow of a cloud passed, even if a red leaf fell outside, she looked out expectantly through the door.

It was middle afternoon when, on looking up, she saw a young woman crossing the porch, leading a little child. Charlotte jumped to her feet, then reseated herself and waited for the tap on the glass. The visitors were strangers to her, and though she could not have told why, as she sat staring at them through the door, her mouth suddenly set into the lines of indomitable obstinacy which had grown so deep around it in the past three years. When she finally crossed the room to open the door, she walked slowly and deliberately, as if she had some definite purpose in mind and meant to accomplish it.

The woman on the outside was the first to speak. "Does Mr. Emory Blake live here?" she asked.

"He does. I am his wife. What can I do for you?" asked Charlotte.

The woman gave a little cry and drew back. "Oh no!" she said, breathlessly.

Charlotte stood, white and stiff and silent, while the other looked about her in a despairing helplessness. She was a frail-looking woman, worn with fatigue and the excited emotions with which timidity spurs itself to action. She looked as if she longed to sit down somewhere, and as if perhaps she could have more courage seated, but Charlotte made no motion to invite her to enter. After a while the newcomer brought her frightened eyes back to the set face in the doorway.

"I am so sorry for you," she said, timidly. "I am his wife."

A shiver of resentment ran convulsively through Charlotte's muscles. "You can be sorry for yourself," she said, roughly.

"But he married me while he was at the school of pharmacy," the other cried, weakly. "I was Nettie Trent. I clerked, and I boarded where he did, and we fell in love and married. He told me about you. You are Charlotte Hastings, aren't you, that wanted to marry him before he left home?"

Charlotte moved her dry lips soundlessly once or twice before she could speak. Then her masterful spirit rose to a new task. She drew herself up and looked down gravely, almost compassionately, upon the woman who had been Nettie Trent.

"I was Charlotte Hastings before my marriage," she said. "I am sorry to be the one to hurt you, but you have been cruelly treated. I was married to Emory Blake before he left home for the school."

The smaller woman gave a little gasp and stood silent, while Charlotte, with the fire in her veins scorching her cheeks and eyes and almost smothering her breath, waited for her to offer some resistance, to assert her own claim, or to ask for proof of the statement which denied it; but Nettie said nothing, and after a moment her gaze dropped from Charlotte's and she began to sob. Charlotte took her by the hand and led her into the room.

Neither of them spoke for a long time. Nettie sat with her face buried in her hands. On one side her child tugged at her dress; on the other, little Hope slept in her cradle. Charlotte stood pale and tall, watching all three.

At last Nettie looked up. "I suppose you think I ought to hate him—now I've found out," she said, "but I don't; I just can't. When we were together he was so sweet to me. I don't think he meant to harm me. He must have thought it would come out all right somehow."

"If I were in your place," Charlotte said, slowly, "I should hate him."

Nettie wiped her eyes and drew her child up into her arms. "But what he did was almost as bad for you as it was for me," she urged, "and you don't hate him."

Charlotte turned suddenly and walked to her own baby's cradle. "Oh, I don't know," she said, in a low voice.

After a moment she came back and sat down. "I must ask you some questions," she said, gravely. "Is this your only child?"

The young woman nodded. Her lips were quivering. "Named Dorcas," she said, brokenly,—"for his mother."

Charlotte flushed and the lines about her lips deepened. "Does he—provide for you?" she asked.

The other nodded once more. "He sends me money once in a while. I wrote him not to worry when he didn't have it. I'm clerking again."

Charlotte made no comment. She was thinking how strange it was that this other woman, who was a frail, poor-spirited thing, should be ready to support herself and child out of love for Blake. In Charlotte's mind, which was pitilessly clear and active, there was room for a passing wonder at the mysterious power which so weak a man could exert over women, even without his will. She was wondering, too, if her own passion for him would ever rise again. At present she was far from loving him; she felt only a bitter resentment, a desire to punish him by holding to him, and a towering obstinacy and pride which refused to be set at fault and put to shame. While she was boldly examining and analyzing herself she glanced at the clock to see how long before he could possibly return; the time was ample, and she continued to sit silent. Presently her baby woke, and she rose and went to it.

As she lifted it from its cradle, Nettie started up and came towards her. Hope hid her face against her mother's neck, but after an instant turned shyly to steal a glance at the stranger.

Nettie sat down again, trembling. "Your baby is like him," she said.

"Very like him," Charlotte answered, and as the baby nestled up to her again, she dropped her cheek against it and tears came into her eyes—scalding tears that seemed to sear their way up from the depths of her heart.

Suddenly the other wife leaned forward, eagerly suspicious. "You have no other children—*older*?" she asked.

Charlotte looked round blankly, her eyes still wet. "*Other* children?" she echoed, but Nettie's sharpened face brought her to herself. She wiped her eyes on Hope's dress. "I lost—a child," she said.

"Oh," Nettie murmured, "I'm sorry I asked you. It was older than Dorcas?"

Charlotte stood at bay, with her child strained close to her. She nodded.

"Oh!" Nettie murmured again, in a shaken voice. She looked at Charlotte in despairing envy. "What is this baby named?" she asked.

"This one," Charlotte answered, "we call Hope."

She seated herself and began trotting the child to a slow measure. There were still a few questions which she wished to ask, but the other's simple acceptance of all she said inspired her with cool deliberation. There was plenty of time, and she wished to make no mistake. She must be sure of her own safety, and after that she must do anything she could for the comfort of the other woman. It would probably be very little.

"How did you get here?" she inquired, finally. "You must have asked somebody where Mr. Blake lived."

"No, I didn't have to ask. He'd written me he was boarding with a woman that lived on his old place," Nettie said, "and I knew where that was because he'd often told me all about where he grew up and just the road he used to take from the station to the house, and I remembered every word of it. I didn't like to go to him at his store for fear there would be loafers around, so I came right to his house. I thought I wouldn't mind telling the woman that I was his wife, if she asked me any questions while I waited for him."

"You were very wise," Charlotte said, dryly.

Nettie settled back in her chair, rocking her little girl, who had grown restless and impatient, and as she rocked she began to pour out her heart. "You must think queer of me to sit down here with you like this and not to be in a rush to go," she began, "but I feel like I've got to sit still and—and kind of get my breath before I can start out. I've been so afraid of it that it doesn't seem like I ought to be surprised, but I tell you it pretty near kills me now I know it for sure." She paused and stroked a stray lock of hair away from her child's eyes. "My baby's like him, too," she said, irrelevantly. "My baby's just as like him as yours is."

Charlotte glanced again at the clock. "How do your friends treat you?" she asked, abruptly. "Do they believe you were really married or not?"

A bright flush sprang over Nettie's face. "They believed it at first, of course, just the way I did," she answered, quickly, "but lately they've been suspecting something. It was what they said made me get uneasy. I don't distrust folks right quick myself."

"And none of them tried to make inquiries for you?"— Charlotte put the question seriously, all her nerves tight strung.

"Oh no," Nettie said. "I don't have any family or any friends close enough to me to take trouble like that."

"And I presume you're glad now that they didn't," Charlotte said. "In your place I'd rather find it out for myself."

"Oh, I'd much rather," Nettie answered. "I couldn't have stood having other people find it out, and I'm not going to give anybody that knows me a chance to find out now. You see, I've been afraid of this so long that I've had time to make my plans and to save up money a little. Before I came here I gave up my place and told folks I was going to join Mr. Blake; so I'll not go back. I'll go to New York and get work there."

Charlotte looked at her keenly. "I suppose you're depending on Mr. Blake to help you?" she said.

Again the color sprang into Nettie's face. "Oh no, ma'am," she answered. "I couldn't let him help me now. I did wrong to live with him, but I didn't know he was married, so I don't feel like one of that kind of women; but if I was to take money from him now, I—I shouldn't feel that I was raising my child honest."

Charlotte lifted her baby so that it hid her face. "For him to help you would only be right," she said, from its shelter. "He owes you—money, at least."

The other shook her head. "I couldn't bear it," she said, chokingly. "Oh, you can't understand—nobody could understand unless she'd been through what I have, being left before my baby came, and having people ask me close questions, and then, little by little, losing my own faith. You can't see why, but if I was to take money from him now, it would make me feel my shame, and I don't want to,—I want to feel honest."

Charlotte lowered Hope to her knee. "Perhaps I can understand that—in a way," she said, with twitching lips.

Nettie looked into her face with a helpless, childish perception of the suffering shown in its drawn lines. "You're so good to me—I believe you feel 'most as bad as I do," she declared; "and if I were you, I wouldn't say a word to anybody about my having been here. Nobody knows it. I didn't have to ask my way. There aren't many women would treat me the way you do, and I won't stay here any longer making you feel bad." She rose, still holding her heavy child in her arms. "There isn't anything more we've got to say to each other, is there?" she asked.

"Wait a moment," Charlotte said. She, too, rose, and as she stood looking at the other woman, so much smaller, so much weaker, so blindly trustful, and so patient, her heart, which had sunk in shame, rose suddenly in pity; at that moment if she had opened her lips the truth would have escaped from them, but her stubborn will held her lips closed.

Nettie eyed her with troubled uncertainty, but after a moment moved towards the door.

"Well, I must go," she declared.

"Wait a moment," Charlotte said again. Her voice was so dry and strange that after she had spoken she paused to moisten her lips. Her limbs trembled, and in the glass door which she had opened against the wall she could see the ashen whiteness of her face.

Nettie turned, and the two women confronted each other, each holding her child.

Charlotte put a hand up to her throat. "I have money I could give you," she offered. "Not his, my own."

The other shook her head. "Oh, I couldn't," she exclaimed. "Anyway, I don't need it. I've saved up a good deal. And you've done better than give me money; you've been kind to me." She put out her hand with a little appealing gesture and took Charlotte's, which lay cold in it.

"You'd better go," Charlotte broke out. "You'll meet him coming home if you wait any longer. Here; I'll tell you how to go a roundabout way."

She walked out on to the piazza and led the way down the steps and round to the back of the house, where she stood giving short, sharp directions, when across her hurried words came Blake's voice calling from the front:

"Charlotte! Charlotte! Where are you and Hope?"

For the first time since they had lived together Blake had come home before his hour.

The two women looked at each other. Charlotte pointed to the path which hid itself quickly in the shelter of an orchard. "Run," she whispered. "I'll keep him in the house."

But Nettie stood as if paralyzed, her eyes widening and filling with tears. "Oh, you've been so good—mayn't I see him—mayn't I bid him good-by?" she begged.

Charlotte lifted her voice to answer Blake. "Yes, Emory; stay where you are; I'm bringing Hope," she called. "Hurry!" she whispered to the other woman. "It won't do you any good to see him. Think of what he's done. Hurry, I say!"

Nettie put her hand up to her head. "I—I can't," she murmured. She swayed a little, and before Charlotte could reach out to catch her she had slipped to the ground.

At the same moment Blake came out of the back door of the house. For an instant he stared in bewilderment. Then he was at Nettie's side and had lifted her in his arms.

Charlotte saw his face as he kissed her. A moment later she was indoors on her knees beside her bed, with her face buried in the cover and her hands clutching it.

A cold wind swept through the house. Front and back the doors stood open. The sun was already low in the west and the evening promised to be chill. Presently Charlotte rose. She closed the front door carefully, wrapped Hope in a cloak, and, with her child on her arm, passed out at the back.

Blake had stretched his wife on the back porch and was bending over her. He looked up, and at sight of Charlotte's face he straightened himself.

She paused an instant. "I'm starting to harness the horse," she said. "You can catch the night train at Antioch if I drive fast."

He stood silent, his face working. It was as if strength were being born in him to say something in his own defence.

"She has plans," Charlotte added. "You'd better pick up some of your things in the house."

She passed on, and laying Hope in the bottom of the wagon, harnessed the horse with swift, shaking hands. The sun was out of sight when she drove back to the house. Nettie sat on the steps staring dazedly around her. Blake was not in sight.

"Are you ready?" Charlotte called.

He came out, carrying an old handbag. At the step he hesitated.

She pointed to the back seat, where he was to sit with Nettie and the child, and after an instant he helped them in.

The ride was long and cold. Night fell, and the stars came out in remote, hostile legions. The children slept. Occasionally Nettie and Blake advised together in hushed voices. Charlotte whipped the horse.

As they drew near to the end of their journey Blake leaned forward and touched her arm.

"What about the store?" he asked.

Charlotte broke her long silence harshly. "Your stock will cover what you owe on it, I guess."

At the station she stayed in the wagon. Blake took his wife

and Dorcas into the waiting-room and came back for his bag. Charlotte had it ready for him, resting on the wheel.

He did not offer to take it at first, but stood in the beam from the station window, trying to speak.

"Well?" she said.

"I guess there's not much I can say," he choked out.

For a long time she made no answer. Then her breath came with an unexpected gasp. "It wasn't your fault—I made you do it." For a moment more they were silent. Then she shifted the sleeping baby towards him.

"Don't you want to kiss her?" she asked.

He bent his face to the child with a sudden passionate tenderness. As he looked up, his wet eyes met Charlotte's, which were full of tears.

She put out her hand to him. "I guess I've been hard on you," she said.

ELIZABETH AND DAVIE

BY MURIEL CAMPBELL DYAR

When the town doctor, coming out to Turkey Ridge, had given as his verdict that Elizabeth's one chance of life—he could not say how slim the chance in that plain room, having within it the pleasant noise of bees and the spring sun on the floor—lay in her going to the great hospital in the city, it was Davie who fell to sobbing in his worn hands.

"I'll jest die at home, Davie," she said in her quiet voice.

"You'll take the money put away for our buryin' an' go, dearie!" Davie cried out fiercely. His gaunt frame, stooped as a scholar's, shook so pitifully with his grief, she had not the heart to gainsay him, but after she promised him it only shook the more.

"Why, Davie," she chided, brightly, "ain't I always been a-wantin' to see the city streets with the hurryin' people, 'n' tall houses, 'n' churches with towers on 'em? They ain't many folks on th' Ridge'll hev sech a lettin'-out as mine."

"If I only had 'nough saved to go too," he mourned.

She answered him simply: "An' who'd I hev to write to me,

with you goin' 'long? It'll seem terrible nice to hear from somebody. I always did love letters. Sence Cousin Tabby died I ain't had one."

"You won't be afeard travellin' so far by yourself?" he asked then, awestruck. Davie had the diffidence of the untravelled. Few men ever left the small farming district of Turkey Ridge for a journey; but if one did so, and the trip were long, he had thereafter a bolder bearing.

"Afeard?" She gave a little trembling laugh which would have deceived no one but a dull old man, now smitten suddenly by sorrow. "The idee o' my bein' afeard! They ain't a mite o' danger o' gettin' run over er lost er nothin'—not a mite."

Under the pretext of bending to hunt for a lost pin she hid the sad fear in her eyes—a fear of all the greater world which was beyond Davie, from whom she had not been parted since her marriage.

But throughout the time of her preparation she went bravely. She would herself have put in order for leaving the house kept spotless even while her disease had crept upon her, but the news of the doctor's words had gone up through the group of farmhouses, huddled like timid sheep on the road, and the kindly neighbor women left their own work, very heavy in the spring-time, to take her household burdens. In a community where no great things ever came save two, and these two birth and death, misfortune drew soul to soul. Because of her gathering weakness she yielded that others should do the tasks which had always hitherto been hers, but she could not be prevented from the packing of the little leather trunk that had held her wedding things. "You're jest makin' me out a foolish, lazy body," she said, her lips seen quivering for the first time. Then, fearful lest she should seem ungrateful for the kindness of her friends, she made haste to ask where, in the trunk, to put her staid, coarse linen, and where her best cap with its fine bow of lavender ribbon, and would they if they were she take her mending-basket along in hopes there might be moments for Davie's socks?

Many a loving offering was tucked in with her belongings to go with her. Now blue-eyed Annie Todd knocked at the door, bringing a bunch of healing herbs from her mother, who could not leave for reason of her nursing baby. Then old Mr. Bayne drove into the dooryard with a pair of knitted bedroom slippers, wrapped carefully in a newspaper. Next Kerrenhappuch Green, perturbed in his long jaw, pottered down to fetch the pinball which his daughter had forgotten when she came to help. Mrs. Glegg, who had lately lost her idiot son, Benje, gave a roll of soft flannel. Miss Panthea Potter contributed a jar of currant jam, three years sealed, and pretended that she was not moved. The minister copied out a verse from the Psalms and fixed it so cunningly about a gold piece that, proud as a girl in her poverty, Elizabeth could not refuse the gentle gift. It was he, too, possessing the advantage of a clerkly hand, who arranged for Elizabeth's admission to the free ward of the hospital, and wrote to his niece Mary, living by good fortune in the city, to have a care over her while there. He told that Mary had a kind, good-humored face, and was herself country born.

"I'll be better able to thank ye all fittenly," the white-haired old woman said, "when I come back to ye well 'n' strong."

The last day before she was to start, all that was possible being done for her, she and Davie were left to themselves, at the minister's suggestion. Forty years before, Davie had brought her to the house, yet in her soft marriage dress. The wedding journey had been the coming up at sunset to the Ridge from her home in the valley, behind his plough-horses, lifting their plodding hoofs as in the furrows. On the clean straw in the back of the wagon rested her small trunk and a hive of bees, shrouded in calico. Tied to the tail-piece was a homesick heifer. While he unhitched the horses and placed her dowry, she entered his door to lay off her bonnet tremulously in the living-room.

Alone with the clumsy carpet-loom which made his winter's work, and his tired week-day hat hanging from a peg against the wall, she had a deep moment. Joining him on the door-step, they sat side by side watching in silence the light die over the scanty fields handed down to him by his father, who had grown bent and weary in wrenching a living from them as he was aging. Neither was young; both were marked by the swift homeliness of the hard-working; but the look on their faces was that which falls when two have gotten an immortal youth and beauty in each other's hearts.

It had been their custom on each succeeding spring to go, if the anniversary ware pleasant, to sit again at evening on the door-step with the sweetness of the straggling spice-bush upon it. Now as they sat there a silence came upon them like that of their wedding-day. Elizabeth broke it first.

"Davie," she whispered, "if I'd say I'd jest like to run through the house a minute by myself, you won't think it queer?"

"No, no," answered Davie, something gripping his chest.

She went slowly, her slippers flapping back and forth on her heels. She sought first the tidy kitchen with its scoured tins, then the living-room with the old loom still in the corner, then the parlor. Here she drew a long, shaken breath. Every Ridge woman loved her parlor with an inherited devotion. Many unrecorded self-sacrifices furnished it. Elizabeth's lay hallowed to her. It was her Place Beautiful. There was a pale, striped paper on the sacred walls, and on the floor an ingrain carpet, dully blue. At the windows were ruffled white curtains—the ruffles and sheer lengths of lawn had lain long in her dreams. The mantel-piece held a row of shells, their delicate pink linings showing, and on either end china vases filled with sprays of plumy grass. Above was the marriage certificate, neatly framed. On the centre-table were sundry piteous ornaments, deeply rooted in her affections. The chairs and the single sofa, angular and sombre, were set about with proud precision. They had been the result of years of careful hoarding of egg-money, and were, to Elizabeth, the achievement of her living.

Holding on to the banister, she climbed the stairs forlornly to the upper chambers. In her own room Davie found her by and by. She was sitting up very straight in her rocker, a baby's long clothes on her lap. Her expression of pain was gone, and in its stead was the strange peace of a woman who sees her first-born. She looked up absently at her husband.

"Melindy Ethel," her voice crooned, "was so little 'n' warm."

"You must jest lay down 'n' rest, dearie," he urged, anxiously. He took the things from her and laid them back, one by one, in the lower drawer of the high, glass-knobbed bureau whence she had taken them. The thin stuff of the little, listless sleeves and yellowed skirts clung to his roughened fingers; he freed them with gentleness.

"An' her hair would hev curled," she said, when the last piece was in.

Davie had been kneeling among his vegetables that summer-time long since that Elizabeth had come to stand beside him in their garden, pushing from her forehead her heavy falling hair, then dark, in the way she had if very glad. Seeing that she had something to tell him, and wondering at her eyes, he waited for her to speak. She did not keep him long. For an instant her serene glance went up to the blue sky. Then her hands stretched out to him.

"Davie," she began, "that old cradle of your ma's—" She broke off shyly.

Davie stayed on his knees. He could not at once answer her, but could only grope toward her blindly. Presently her touch calmed him.

"It rocks from head to foot," he quavered in joy, "'stead o' from side to side—the motion's better for 'em."

Striving to go well through her troubled months until her hour should come, Elizabeth smiled often at Davie, and sometimes the smile was a tender laugh in her throat—Davie clumping excitedly over the farm about his work; Davie bringing home from town the cautious purchase of a child's sack, and crying out in exultation, "It's got tossels on it!" Davie storing singular treasures in a box in the garret—seed-pods which rattled when you shook them; scarlet wood-berries, gay and likely to please; a tin whistle, a rubber ball, a doll with joints, and a folded paper having written on it, "For Croup a poultis of onions and heeting the feet"; and Davie, his importance dropped from him as a garment, coming to put his head down against her shoulder.

"I dun'no'," he said to her, "as a man better feel too uppity 'bout becomin' a pa. It's an awful solemn undertakin', an' the more you think it over the solemner it gets. Seems to me it's somethin' like playin' the fiddle. There can't jest anybody rush in an' play a real good time on a fiddle—takes a terrible lot o' preparin' 'n' hard work to tech them little strings to music. An' mebbe the man that can tech 'em the best is him that's always been clean 'n' honest 'n' real grave. I'm beginnin' to feel so no 'count—why, I dun'no' a note o' fiddle music!"

"Oh, Davie," she had comforted, "it don't seem to me that the man jest *born* good 'd play the sweetest, but the one who had fought for things."

While she turned the tiny hems and ran the wonderful seams, Davie, winter-bound, sat on the tall stool before his loom, the bobbins wound with rags for a hit and miss. Weaving eked out a slender income. His father's finger-tips, too, had become stained by colors of warp and woof after the end of the pig-killing had been announced by the children racing with the bladders through the thin snow.

On Christmas day he brought down the cradle from the garret, and wiped its gathered dust from it with a white cloth. To please him, Elizabeth spread it ready with the sheets and blankets. The sight of the pillow unmanned him. "The idee o' that stove smokin' so Christmas!" he choked. She turned to him quickly. Their seamed hands met as in that joyous moment among the vegetables, but this time they clasped above a dusted cradle. In view of the increased expenses before the household they made each other no gifts; only Davie put a fir bough and a teething-ring in his box.

Then he wove as though the clack of his shuttle were the beat of a drum going by, then in a vast impatience, then with the bridle hanging on the rim of the manger by the plough-horse which had a saddle gait.

The morning that he clambered, frightened, into the saddle a great cold wave was on the Ridge, with a fierce wind continually blowing. Smoke curled up from the chimneys to perish against the sunny sky. Cattle left in the open crowded in the lee of the straw-stacks, their rough flanks crawling, and in the folds the ewes, yet frail from their travail, stood stung and still, mothering their weak-kneed lambs. Beside the thud of the horse's hoofs toward town there was no sound on the road save a little, dry cracking of the frost. The doctor, as he started in his carriage for Davie's house, drew his robes closely about him and scowled at the fierceness of the blast; but Davie, riding far ahead, his elbows flying wildly up and down, did not know that he had forgotten to fasten his shabby overcoat. Crouched by the silent loom, he clutched helplessly at the hit and miss as Elizabeth went down into that loneliest of all earth's agonies.

But from the beginning the child hung a doomed thing on her breast. After three months they followed her up to the burying-ground, the murmuring of its cedars never again to be wholly out of their ears. Away from the grave Davie gave an exceedingly bitter cry—"She's little to leave!" But Elizabeth's tears fell back in her heart unshed. She waved her handkerchief to Melindy Ethel. "But she's brave like her pa," she said. And Davie stiffened.

Memories of these and other days, mingled with forebodings for the parting, were so heavy upon him that he could get no farther in the night's devotions than the reading of the Bible chapter.

"I can't pray to-night, 'Lisbeth," he said.

Propped with pillows for the last rest before her journey, she was still faithfully brave. "Mebbe the Lord'll jest take care o' me, anyway, bein' as I've tried to do his ways." The old man did not know how wistful was her speech.

In the morning she was early dressed in her decent black. To those who came for the leave-taking she bade good-by with gentle courtesy. Kerrenhappuch Green lent his buggy because of its comfortable seat, but Davie drove her carefully over the six miles to the station. No shriek of an engine's whistle disturbed the quiet of Turkey Ridge; to go into wider ways one must needs start from the nearest town. Once she looked back at the house, set like an ancient brown bird's nest on the narrow fields.

The yellow-bodied stage, going every other day across the country, brought the minister the letter from his niece with the happy tidings of Elizabeth's safe arrival, under her guidance, at the city hospital. The stage-driver viewed the missive with professional interest as he delivered it. The majority of his passengers paid him monotonously in butter or eggs for his services, his trips were tedious, and his ideals were limited. To read and digest all postals and to conjecture at the contents of all envelopes were his reward for handing out the mail at the turning of the lanes. The minister jogged down instantly to Davie's in his sulky, slapping the lines vigorously, if ineffectually, over the back of his brown mare, which understood, with a truly feminine insight, his perplexity before her character. Davie dropped his hoe and ran stumbling to meet him. He read the pages in a tremble. There was something for him from Elizabeth at the bottom of the last one. "Dear Davie," it ran, "are you well an' lookin' jest the same? Don't get lonesome for me. I ain't missin' you a mite."

During the period that she was resting for the operation Mary wrote daily, and every time the letter came the minister jogged down to the farmhouse, for the words were really from the old wife to Davie. Very cheerful words they were for the most part. "If Davie's askin' how the streets look, tell him I can't jest tell, for I come in the night, but the noise is amazin'." "Tell Davie I can see a church tower from the window, an' it's higher 'n' we ever dreamt of its bein', an' sweeter." "Tell Davie to lay listenin' to feet goin' up and down on stones is grand." "Tell Davie I hev seen the surgeon an' that I never thought a great man'd be so kind. I was all in a flutter over him, but when he'd come 'n' had seen me, whatever'd I do but tell him 'bout him 'n' Melindy Ethel, an' the meetin'-house, an' how the road runs by in front o' the farm. An' he said he knew, an' not to mind—as ma ust to. Ain't it strange 'bout his knowin'?"

The letters to Elizabeth were a tremendous labor, for Davie was no speller, and always bashful in the presence of ink. He had only little happenings for his pen—he wrote with his tongue forming the painful syllables about his mouth. But to her they were infinite things—the May rose was blossomed in the garden, and a pair of robins were nesting on a ledge of the loom on finding the room so still; the speckled hen scratched up the pease, and the black cow's calf was lamed; the house dog pined for her and whimpered at the doors, letting the cats lick the edges of his dish; the neighbors had sent donations of a loaf of rye bread, a pitcher of broth, and the half of a new pressed cheese; Kerrenhappuch Green sat with him in the evenings, and he, Davie, was not getting lonesome nor missing *her* at all. But the one blotted "'Lisbeth, 'Lisbeth," told the true tale of the empty house.

When no letter came from Mary he toiled, white as lint, in his potato-field. There followed two days of sick suspense; then the minister waved to him at the gray fence-rails. So greatly did he dread to hear the news he longed to know, he could not stir from the spot where he stood, but waited, a strained, pathetic figure, for him to make his way across the even furrows. On the fatherly, near-sighted countenance, as he drew nearer, was to be seen such a shining brightness that straightway Davie knew that she whom he loved had issued from her trial. The two men, alike weather-beaten and seamed by a humble work—the shepherd no less than the sheep of his flock anxiously tilling a rocky farm,—had the reticence which is learned in hill solitudes, but in the "Thank God, Davie," and the breaking "Yes, sir," much was spoken.

Now Davie slackened his toil and opened all the windows of the house to freshen the low-ceilinged rooms for Elizabeth's returning. Every morning he picked bunches of spring flowers and arranged them in stiff bouquets on the tables and old bureaus. He took out his Sunday suit from the closet and rebrushed it carefully and laid it with a clean collar and his musty tie. He began to carry himself all at once with something of an air, and he developed a reckless and unnatural enthusiasm about the weather; for to be darkly critical of the season after the thaw was a local point of masculine etiquette which hitherto he had scrupulously observed. The spring had always been in his judgment, sympathetically received, "too terrible warm," or "pointin' right to a late frost that'll kill everything," or, were it not palpably a failure, "so durned nice now that the summer'll be mean." But with the good news coming from the hospital he was ready to declare in response to friendly greetings: "It's the beatin'est time I ever come 'cross. Dun'no' when I hev heerd so many bluebirds or sech chirky ones. An' the sky's wonderful an' the ground's jest right. It's goin' to be a dreadful good year for farmin'."

There was in his mind no premonition of trouble on his receiving from the lumbering stage an envelope directed to him in Elizabeth's own hand. It was only that she was getting able to write to him herself. He took it unopened up to the bench by the May rose to read its contents at his leisure away from the stage-driver's curious gaze. "Dear Davie," the letter said, "the city streets is so wearyin' an' I'm comin' home. If I ain't so well as we hoped, don't mind. 'Tain't like I was young to leave. Mary's comin' with me, for she's long been wantin' to visit the Ridge. Could you meet me with your wagon, Davie?"

She could not tell, what she did not know, that the money for Mary's journey had been sent to her by the minister for his old friend's needs.

*   *   *   *   *

The afternoon was very soft and fair when Davie met the train incoming to town from the city. The farms on Turkey Ridge were illumined with growing things like the faint, precious pages of a missal. Doves fluttered on the lowly roofs. Everywhere was the calling of birds and the smell of broken earth. The minister and Mary fell behind along the way. Kerrenhappuch Green, caught walking westward to the creek, his stale pockets bulged by bait, hid with a simple delicacy in the roadside bushes from Davie's face. Only the children hastening from school nodded to him as he passed them, nor hushed the loud clatter of their burring tongues.

It was not for young children to be stricken by that sight upon the road—the pair of patient horses drawing slowly homeward in the shining of the sun a wagon fresh lined with straw, on which lay a homely mother, smiling with old lips; and above her, on the seat, humbly bowed in his Sunday suit, a gray-haired man whose cheeks were wet with tears.

BARNEY DOON, BRAGGART

BY PHILIP VERRILL MIGHELS

The nine dusty citizens of Bitter Hole, having one and all proposed, unsuccessfully, for the hand of Miss Sally Wooster, had about concluded that Bitter Water Valley was a desert, after all, when they finally thought to turn their attention once again to Barney Doon, the cook.

Let it here be stated, nevertheless, there was one thing to prove that the valley was a desert, despite the presence of Barney, and that was the face of the country itself. One-half of that whole Nevada area was a great white blister, forty miles long and fifteen wide, acrid with alkali, flat, barren, and harsh as a sheet of zinc. The valley's remaining territory was covered with gray, dry scrub, four inches high, through which the dusty Overland stage-route was crookedly scratched.

Bitter Hole was the station for the stage. In it flourished the nine dusty citizens, a dusty dog, and a dusty chicken, in addition to Barney and the buxom Miss Sally, whose father was among the citizens enumerated. At the end of the street was a hole, or well, the waters of which, being not precisely fatal to men and horses, had occasioned the growth of the place, there being no other water for leagues along the road.

Here in this land, even when Sally had scorned them, each in turn, the men of the Hole were still agreed there could be no desolation where Barney Doon had residence. Purely and simply they loved the little cook for the fiery suddenness of his temper and the ingenuity of the insults of which he was never guiltless. The sulphurous little demon was, as the miners and teamsters estimated, "only two sizes bigger than a full-grown jack-rabbit." What he lacked in size, however, he more than supplied in expression of countenance. His eyes were centres of incandescence, while the meagre supply of hair he grew bristled redly out from beside his ears like ill-ordered spears. Indeed, such a red-whiskered, bald-headed little parcel of fireworks as Barney was is rarely created.

Calmly considered, it is hardly a matter for marvel that Barney had, from time to time, accommodated every individual in the Hole with a quarrel. Moreover, he had challenged each to mortal combat. Indeed, he had never been known to do anything less. Barney was a challenger first and a cook incidentally. But, ancient and modern tradition through, there never was chronicle of actual encounter in which the fierce little cook cut figure.

And, as a matter of fact, the men esteemed him perhaps somewhat more for the skill and adroitness with which he invariably squirmed out of impending engagements, than they did for all the alacrity and pyrotechnics with which he was wont to surround himself with duelsome entanglements. The boys well knew that if blood were unlet till the bragging, hot little rogue of a Barney stained his record, they would all forget the color of a wound.

It was not without some elemental enthusiasm that the camp, one evening, extended its welcome to a mule-driver newly mustered to their company. The sobriquet by which the man was duly introduced was Slivers. He was swiftly appraised and as quickly assimilated, after which there was only one process required to complete his initiation, namely, that of preparing his mind for a "racket" with Barney Doon.

"Don't lose no time, but git right in at supper," instructed John Tuttle, for the group. "Jest bang him with any old insult you can think of, and leave the rest to Barney. Trot out a plain, home-made slap at the fodder he's dishin' up, fer instance. And when he comes at you with a challenge, don't fergit your privilege of pickin' out the weapons—savvy?"

It chanced that the moment selected for the entertainment was most propitious, inasmuch as Barney had that day declared his devotion to Sally Wooster, and had duly desired her big red hand for his own, only to hear a wild peal of laughter in reply, and to find himself boosted bodily out of the window by the hearty young lady herself. He was not, therefore, exactly in a mood of milk and honey.

It never had failed, and it did not fail to-night, that Barney should conceive himself more than half insulted merely by the sight of a stranger appearing at the board and calmly requiring the wherewithal to satisfy a mountain appetite. Accordingly, when the miners and teamsters all came filing in, dusty, angular, raw-looking of countenance, Barney instantly detected the presence of Slivers among them, and his eyes "lit up shop" without delay.

Slivers, to speak the truth, was easily seen. He was framed like a sky-scraping building, with the girders all plainly suggested. Not without a certain insolence of deliberation, he stared about the room before assuming his seat, and provoked himself to a sneer of opera-bouffe proportions.

"You're his meat already," whispered one of the men. "Set down."

Comrade Slivers thereupon proceeded to comport himself with a studied indifference to the cook which was duly galling. In a grim silence that all who knew him comprehended, Barney went about the table glowering with ferocity. Edging closer and closer to Slivers, the little man seemed itching in his ears to catch some careless word that might, by dint of inventiveness, be construed as a personal affront.

"I can see you ain't got no cook in the camp," said Slivers, loudly, to his neighbor, when Barney was directly behind his chair. "Has that pizened little boy I seen a while ago been playin' keep-house with the grub?"

"What's the matter with the grub, you scion of the wild-ass family?" demanded Barney, exploding like a fulminate.

Slivers looked around and scowled. "Git out, you yawping brat," said he. "You must have been losin' hair for years—one hair a day—for everything you don't know about decent grub. Go look at yer head, and figure out your ignorance."

Sensitive concerning the trackless Sahara which his pate presented, Barney clapped his hand upon it instantly. He could scarcely speak, for rage.

"You—dead lizard!" finally spurted from his safety-valve. "You mongrel viper! Low-bred ooze, disowned and outcast, I'll spoil a grave with your carcass for this! You jelly of cowardice, meet me to-morrow for satisfaction, or I'll swing you about by the tongue, and hurl you to pulp against the sty of a pig!"

Even Slivers somewhat gasped.

"Meet you?" he retorted, arising, to tower above his foeman like a mast. "Iron me, Johnny!—if I can crawl in the hole to find you where you're hidin' I'll make you wish for hair a mile long, to stand on your head in your pitiful scare!"

"Oh, fie! Oh, bah!" said the cook, scanning the teamster's length with ill-concealed awe. "Buzzard, you toy with languages. To-morrow I shall throw tomato-cans in scorn to build your monument."

"All right," answered Slivers. "To-morrow suits me, and we'll fight it out bareback on buckin' broncos, out in the small corral, each feller armed with a stockin' full of rocks for a weapon."

Barney stared for a moment in consternation at the man before him. He had previously grown accustomed to the horrors suggested by pistols, knives, red-hot branding-irons, and even pitchforks, but rocks in a stocking—that smacked of barbarism. Moreover, to mount on the back of a bronco, wild or tame—the very meditation made the walls drop out of his stomach. However, he smiled.

"Child's play!" he answered, with fine disgust. "You warty infant! No matter, an odious child would become a more detestable reptile! Till to-morrow, don't speak to me—don't speak to me! Or I shall cheat myself of the morning's pastime." And with that he strode haughtily away.

"Howlin' coyotes!" said Slivers, when he met the gaze of a dozen pair of gleaming eyes. "Take him dose for dose he's worse than pizen! By gar! just see if he burned any holes in my shirt."

Nearly all night long, however, little Barney lay awake, wildly fashioning excuses to avoid that horrid duel in the morning. He had always escaped by a margin so narrow that no precedent of the past gave assurance of luck for the future. He was mortally afraid that at last he had challenged such a monster of brute courage, malignity, and strength that nothing terrestrial could avert his untimely demise.

Then in the morning the first sight that met his troubled gaze was that of Slivers rounding up a pair of unbroken ponies, as wild as meteors, in the field of honor, hard by the camp. Every cell in Barney's structure was in a panic. How he managed to walk to the water-bench to wash was more than he knew. After that there was no retreat. The citizens of Bitter Hole surrounded him, according to preconcerted arrangement, and began to coach him for his fight.

"Barney, you'd better have a jolt of whiskey in yer vitals," suggested one. "Slivers is a regular expert with a stockin' of rocks."

"If I was you, Barney," said Tuttle, "I'd leave my bronco throw me right at him. Then. I'd turn in the air and soak my heels into Slivers's grub-basket and knock him into pieces small enough to smoke in a cigarette."

"Barney," counselled another, "you take my advice and fight standin' up on your hoss, so you can jump over onto Slivers's bronco and cram your stockin' of rocks down that there mule-driver's neck and choke him clean to death."

They were "herding" the speechless Barney toward the corral, in which the two vicious ponies had now been confined. Slivers himself came forward.

"Leave me see how much the little scarecrow has shrunk in the night," said he.

Barney's wrath was kindled by this. He opened his mouth to deliver a broadside of verbal grape and canister, when he was suddenly interrupted.

A shot and a yell, from down the road, startled every man in camp. Two, three, five more shots barked in swift succession. Miss Sally Wooster herself was drawn from the house by the fusillade.

With Comanche-like whoops, a horseman came dashing madly toward the men, brandishing two huge revolvers as he rode.

"Skete, and drunk in the morning," said Tuttle.

A moment later the rider scattered the population as he rode his weltering pony through the group.

"You lubbers, celebrate!" he yelled, discharging a weapon three times in a second. "There's been a baby born at Red Shirt Canyon! We git in the census! We git on the map! Big Matt Sullivan's wife has got a little boy!"

"A boy!" said Sally Wooster. "Oh my!"

"Is that all?" inquired John Tuttle, on behalf of his somewhat indignant townsmen. "Red Shirt's thirty-seven miles away. We've got something more exciting than that right here in camp."

"Red Shirt's in this same county," protested the horseman, a trifle crestfallen. "I thought you fellers was patriotic."

Barney Doon threw out his chest and swaggered forward.

"Patriotic?" he echoed. "Doggone us, we're the biggest patriots on the coast! No man is a gentleman who wouldn't be a gentleman on such an occasion as this. Skete, you've saved the life of yonder braggart," and he pointed to Slivers. "I couldn't be a gentleman and slay him when a child's been born in this here county. Slivers, you can go your way, without alarm."

"What!" demanded Tuttle. "No fight? All on account of a baby?"

"If I ever!" added Sally Wooster.

A third disgusted person queried, "What's a baby got to do with a duel, and the kid near forty miles away?"

To this one Barney turned with pitying scorn. "You don't know how easy it is to disturb a new-born baby," said he. "There ain't a man but me in camp knows how to behave himself in a holy moment like this here, and I ain't a-goin' to kill no man when a sacred thing like that has went and happened."

"Well, durn his slippery hide!" grumbled Tuttle. "He's gittin' too smart!"

The men were all grinning, including Slivers.

"I reckon Barney knows as much about a baby as a hop-toad knows about arithmetic," said Wooster, winking prodigiously. "He's got us all square beat on kids."

"I don't know about that," replied a lanky individual who had sobered amazingly at the news from Red Shirt Canyon. "I've saw a kid or two myself."

"That so, Moody?" said Slivers. "Well, say, maybe we could work up a bet between you and Barney, to see which knows the most about a youngster."

Barney broke in abruptly. "I'll bet a million dollars I know more about children than all you cusses put together! There ain't a one of you knows how many teeth a baby's got when he's born."

The challenge produced a solemn stillness.

"W-e-l-l, I know they don't git their eyes open for a week," asserted Moody.

"You're clear off, first crack," retorted Barney. "It's nine days, instead of a week."

Again the men were awed to silence.

"Yes, that's right—Barney's correct," presently admitted citizen Wooster.

"You old ninnies!" said his daughter Sally, and she turned away to go to the house.

"Well, anyway," said Slivers, after a brisk bit of widespread conversation with Tuttle, "we've got a scheme. Barney wants to match himself against the whole shebang in knowin' about a kid, and we're goin' to fetch a young un to the Hole and leave him prove his claim."

"Not Sullivan's?" gasped Barney, suddenly overwhelmed at the prospect of proving his erudition on an infant so tender, with a father so brawny.

"Never mind whose," replied the teamster. "You sit quiet and look pretty, and we'll provide the kid."

This they did. The following morning, at daylight, Tuttle and Slivers reappeared at camp, from a pilgrimage, and the mule-driver held in his arms a little red Indian papoose, as fat, dimpled, and pretty as a cherub, and as frightened as a captive baby rabbit.

"Now, then," said the man, placing his charge on the floor, in the midst of a circle of wondering citizens, "there's your kid. Never mind where we got him—there he is. Barney takes charge of him every other day, and the rest of us by turns in between—all that cares to enter the race."

The news having spread, Miss Sally Wooster was among the astonished spectators who beheld the tiny, half-naked, frightened little chieftain-to-be, gazing timidly about him as he sat on the planks, gripping his own little shirt as his one and only acquaintance.

"Lauk!" she said, and laughing immoderately, sped for the door.

"Sally, you ain't to help neither Barney nor us!" called Tuttle.

"Don't you worry," she answered. "It ain't no pie of mine."

The men continued to look at their "young un" in no small quandary of helplessness.

"He's a pretty little cuss," said one of the miners, after a moment. "I wouldn't guess him for more than a yearlin'."

Moody coughed nervously. "One of the first things to do for a child," he ventured, "is to git a thimble to rub on his teeth."

"That's right," said a friend. "My mother used to do that regular."

"What's the matter with putting pants on him fairly early in the fight?" inquired the next man of wisdom.

"First thing my mother always done for us was to make us a bib," drawled one fidgety fellow, tentatively.

"He'd orter be told never to drink, ner chew, ner smoke, ner swear, ner gamble, 'fore it gits too late," added a miner who carefully eschewed all and sundry of these virtues.

"Stub-tailed idiots!" said Barney, in huge disgust.

All eyes focussed on the fiery little cook.

"Well, then," demanded Tuttle, "what is the first thing to do for a little kid like him?"

"The first thing?" answered Barney. "The first thing is—Do you think I'm going to tell you lop-eared galoots all I know about a baby? What I want to know is if he's had a bite to eat?"

"What did you think we'd feed him?" asked Slivers. "Do we look like his mother?"

"Git away, you venomous scum, and let me have him!" demanded Barney.

"Hold on," interrupted Tuttle. "The first day he goes to the feller he picks out himself, only you come last, bein' the challenger. We'll arrange things alphabetical. Adams, you git first shot, to find out if you're popular with the little skeesicks."

Adams turned redder than usual, which is saying much.

"Ah—I don't know nuthin' about kids," he confessed.

"Catherwood—see what he can do."

Catherwood also proved to be modest. After him Farnham and Lane waived their alphabetical privilege.

Moody, as nervous as a girl, approached the dumb little man on the floor, and twisting the corner of his coat, inquired in a trembling voice, "Does Bunny love old Goo-goo?"

The child looked up with a frightened little query in his eyes.

"I'd hate to scare him," Moody added. "I don't mind seein' how he takes to Barney."

"Yes, give Barney a show," said Wooster.

Something had been happening to the cook. The tenseness had gone from his usually wiry little body; his eyes were milder; a curve was softening his mouth. Kneeling before the child, he held forth his arms.

"Baby want to go by-by?" he said, and tenderly lifting the little man, he bore him away, while the men looked on in silence.

Half an hour later the man who peeked through the keyhole reported that Barney was singing the youngster to sleep. The words of the song are not readily conveyed, but they sounded like—

"Allonsum sum-sum bill-din,
Allonsum sum-sum bill-din,
Allonsum sum-sum bill-din,"

repeated times without number. Barney called it an Indian lullaby. As sung it was equally good Cherokee, Chinese, or

Russian, being Barney's clearest recollection and inter-pretation of a song which his mother once had droned.

On the third day following, Slivers, Tuttle, and others held a council of war.

"Barney's goin' to clean up the whole works of us," said the mule-driver, "unless we can manage to work some better combination."

"What can we do?" inquired Tuttle. "The kid sure likes him best."

"That wasn't the point. It's a game of how much we all know about a young un as against little Barney. Now, Moody, on the square, do you think you know as much as him?"

"He knows more than you'd think," confessed Moody. "The—the only little kid I ever had—she died—ten months old."

"Oh."

"Well—that was hell, sure."

Some of the men puckered their lips as if to whistle, but made no sound.

"If only we could paint Barney's face an Irish green, or do something so's the kid would be scared to see him, we might win out yet, perhaps," resumed Slivers, presently. "Got any ideas?"

"I don't think Barney could scare him if he tried," answered Wooster. "Anyhow the pore little scamp ain't cried since he come."

"He ain't laughed any, either," added Moody.

There was neither a cry nor a smile that day, though Barney yearned to hear either one of these baby sounds. The little brown captive clung as always to his tiny shirt, and watched Barney's face with big, brown, questioning eyes. The cook had forgotten his boast. To hold the wee bit of babyhood against his heart, to coax him to eat, to yearn over him, love him, fondle him—these were his passions. A fierce parental jealousy grew in Barney's nature.

But the hour arrived when jealousy changed to a deeper emotion—to worry. All Barney actually knew of a child came through the intuitions of a natural father's heart, but little as this amounted to, Barney was aware that a tiny scamp like this should eat and sleep and creep about and crow. And the little brown "Bunny" had done not one of the pretty baby tricks.

The fiery little cook's new concern was at first concealed. With growing reluctance every time, he resigned the little man to Moody's care as the "contest" required. One night, however, when the dumb, sad bit of an Indian was with Moody, the man was aroused from his dreams by some one's presence. It was Barney, too worried to sleep, surreptitiously come to the tiny captive's fruit-box cradle, and gently urging the wee bronze man to eat of some gruel prepared at that silent hour of the darkness. He was willing that Moody should have the credit of taking good care of the motherless baby, if only the child could be made a little more happy. Thereafter, by night and day, the cook was hovering about the uncomplaining little chieftain; and Moody understood.

By some of the mystic workings of nature, Barney's love and worry extended to Sally. Hiding her feelings from all the men, even from Barney himself, she could not quell the upgush of emotion in her bosom, as she snatched the little Indian once, in secret, to her heart. Without the courage, as yet, to hear the men ridicule her weakness, she nevertheless contrived to place a hundred little comforting things in Barney's path, as he went his rounds of mothering his sad little wild thing from the hills. Her heart began to ache, as it swelled to take in the child and Barney Doon.

The men had lost all spirit of fun in the contest, even to Slivers, who strove, however, to see it through in a bluff, rough-hearted way.

Unexpectedly all of it came to a crisis. It was early in the morning. After a sleepless night Barney had gone in desperate parent-care to receive his foundling back from Moody. In one keen glance he had finally perceived what all their folly was leading to, at last.

With the dumb little chap on his arm he hastened to the dining-shed, where all the men, save Tuttle, were awaiting breakfast.

"You brutes had no right to steal this child!" he cried out, passionately. "He's starving! He's pining away! Look at his thin little legs! Look at his poor little eyes—getting hollow!" Tears were streaming from his own tired eyes as he spoke. "Slivers, you did this!" he charged, angrily. "You tell me where you got him, or I'll shoot you down like a dog!" He had hastened up to the teamster, against whose very breast he thrust a pistol a foot in length.

"By God! he'd do it!" said Slivers, unmoved by the push of the loaded weapon. "Uncock it, Barney. You'd ought to know I wouldn't harm the kid, any quicker than you. I'd do as much as any man if we had to save his life."

"He may not live through the day!" cried Barney. "I'm going to take him home—back to his mother! And if you don't tell me where she is—"

"Hold on, now; I call," interrupted Slivers. "We'll see if you've got any sand. The Injun camp is over across the desert, in Thimbleberry Cove.... Do you reckon you've got the nerve to pack him across?"

A peculiar silence followed this announcement. Barney stood like an animal at bay. His face became deathly white. He fully comprehended the awfulness of that great white dead-land just outside.

Wooster broke the silence. "It looks as if the wind is going to blow harder to-day," he said. "It's stirring up the desert some already. A man could never get two miles out from here, unless the breeze goes down."

Barney, with a crazed, wild look on his face, hastened away to the kitchen.

"I'm glad he didn't take you up on that," said Moody, gazing forth from a window. "Get on to the way the whirlwinds are kickin' up the smoke already."

"I reckon it won't blow no worse than yesterday," replied Slivers. "But I knowed he wouldn't tackle it anyhow. He'll be back here in a minute, to squirm out of the game."

They drummed on the table for fifteen minutes, as they waited. A brisk wind was blowing; the desert began to deliver up its cohorts of dust-clouds, where powdered alkali billowed and eddied and swept across the valley in ever-increasing volumes.

"Peek in the kitchen and see what Barney's up to now," prompted Slivers, nudging Adams as he spoke.

"Oh, he'll be back directly," said Adams.

"Here's somebody comin' now," added Catherwood, presently. "Maybe it's—"

"Sally," muttered Slivers, who meditated proposing for the hand of the buxom Miss Wooster.

She came toward them almost fiercely. Her face was white. She too had detected the change come upon the tiny Indian captive. All night she had accused herself of neglect and heartlessness.

"Where's Barney? Where's the baby?" she demanded.

"Barney's maybe striking off for Thimbleberry Cove," answered Slivers, smilingly. "He was running a bluff on taking the kid to its mother."

"But Tuttle told me the mother's up at Red Shirt Canyon," said the girl.

"Of course," agreed Slivers, uneasily. "We—told him about the Cove to test his sand."

Sally gazed at him wildly. "Then—it must have been a man— Barney!—I saw—on the desert!" she cried, disjointedly. "They'll die! Oh no, he wouldn't—" She ran outside to scan the fearful expanse of alkali, with its gathering blizzard of dust.

The men, suddenly grown nervous, followed her out of the house. Apparently there was nothing, far or wide, on the desert, save the sweeping clouds of white, like drifting snow.

"My God! he wouldn't tackle that!" said Slivers.

"I hear some one out in the kitchen now," said Tate. "It must be him."

Sally ran to see. It was only the dog. She darted forth once more.

"Not there!" she said. "But surely Barney wouldn't—There! There!"

Her cry rang out so shrilly that even Slivers started. She was pointing stiffly. The men all stared at the storm of dust. For one brief second the swirling clouds were reft, revealing, far out eastward, in the dead-land of white, a small dark object—the form of a man.

One poignant sob was the only sound that Sally made, as she ran toward the stable.

"Good Lord! it's him!" said Adams. "Was he heading back this way?"

"I think he was," answered Catherwood.

"He couldn't—do anything—else," stammered Slivers.

For a moment no one spoke.

"I reckon I'll just mosey over to the desert," drawled the fidgety man. "I'd hate to have anything go wrong with Barney."

"Guess I'll go along myself," said Adams.

"Boys!" said Slivers, hoarsely, "I'm going to saddle up and git him back! I didn't mean no harm when I told him wrong. I didn't think he'd go. I'd ride through hell for Barney—or the little Injun, either. You fellers know I didn't mean no harm."

He started at once to get his horse. Before he had covered half the distance to the stable, Sally suddenly rode forth, bareback, on a buckskin pony, and heading for the desert, spurred her bronco to a gallop, crying to him wildly as she went.

"Sally!—Sally—I'll go!" yelled Slivers.

She seemed not to hear, but ran her pony out upon the white expanse, where the wreathing dust seemed to swallow both herself and the animal immediately.

Her horse, fleeing swiftly before the wind, carried Sally a mile or two out from the camp before she reined him in. Believing Barney could have come no farther than this, she began to search and to call.

At every turn of her head her eyes were blinded by the acrid dust. The stuff choked her breathing; already her throat was dry. Dust and powder and snow-of-alkali came from every-where. It was blowing up her sleeves. It filtered into and through her clothing. Her ears were quickly coated; her hair was heavy.

She turned her head from side to side for a breath. The air was thicker than smoke with dust as heavy as flour.

"Barney!" she called, from time to time, but the alkali coated her tongue. On either side she could see for a distance of twenty feet, or less. It seemed far less, in all that terrible drift of white.

She rode across the wind, doggedly, crying Barney's name. A nameless hopelessness began to grow upon her. Now this way, now that, she urged her horse. How far could Barney hear her calling? How far could he wander? How far would she ride? There were forty miles in length and fifteen in width of this reek of wind-driven alkali. God keep them if ever they got more than two miles away from the Hole!

It was aimless riding, presently, but she still persisted. A sickening conviction that Barney and the little captive would both be dead before she could find them made her desperation unendurable. With eyes starting hotly, with every breath seeming like a struggle for existence, in the dust, she galloped, calling, calling, till at last she could call no more.

Dazed, she halted her horse at last, and sat staring blindly at nothing. The pony turned about, unheeded, and began to fight his way against the storm, his head down between his legs.

Sally's head also came down, by instinct more than by design. She felt past thinking. For a time she rode thus, heedlessly. Then abruptly she clutched at the reins and drew the horse to a halt. The animal pricked up his ears peculiarly.

Weirdly out of the wind and dust came a sound—not a moan, not a croon, but like them both, yet a song, uncertain, apparently coming from no definitive point. She even caught the words:

"All on some lonesome bill-din
The swallow makes her nest;

All on some—lonesome bill-din
The—swallow makes—her nest."

Sally tried to call out. She made but a croaking noise. Slipping from her horse's back, she groped her way forward, leading the pony, and trying to shout.

For a rod or more she battled against the driving dust, then halted as before. Not another sound would the desert render up—only the strange dry swishing by of the particles of stuff rasping the desert's surface as they passed and rose.

"Barney!" she called, by a mighty effort. There was no response.

Crying now, in her anguish and plight, she led the pony this way and that, up and down, listening, trying to force a shout through her swollen lips. At length, in despair, she knew she could search no more. A lifelessness of feeling was creeping upon her. Mechanically she walked beside her pony, and it was the animal that was leading.

It seemed as if she had plodded onward thus for hours, when at length she stumbled upon a gray little mound in the drifting alkali.

"Barney!" she said, in a voice scarcely more than a whisper. Crooning and sobbing, she lifted him up—unconscious, but clinging to the still, little form that was hugged to the shelter of his breast.

"Hang on—oh, hang on to the horse, dear, please," she coaxed, in all the tender strength of a new-born love. "Barney—try—try, dear, please. I'll be your wife—I'll do anything—if only you'll try."

She had raised him bodily to the pony's back. Stiffly as a man that freezes he straddled the animal. He made no answer, no movement. She feared he must be dead. She dared not look at the little papoose. Barney's weight rested partially upon her shoulder. She tossed away the reins.

"Go on, Sancho—go on home," she croaked to the horse, passionately.

The pony seemed to comprehend. With some faint fragrance of the waters of Bitter Hole in his nostrils, the willing creature fought slowly, steadily forward, against the terrible drift.

* * * * *

John Tuttle and Henry Wooster descried a group, like a sculpture in whitened stone endowed with life, creep strangely out from the blizzard of alkali. A blinded horse, with head bent low, bearing on its back a motionless man, and led by a stumbling, blinded girl, against whose shoulder the helpless rider leaned, came with ghostlike slowness and silence toward them.

And all day long, one by one, more men came forth, like ghosts, from the dead-land. But the twilight had come and the wind had died away before teamster Slivers limped from the desert. He came afoot. He had ridden his horse to death, in his desperate quest. He could barely see—and his hair was white, even below the coating of the dust.

Moody ran to meet him.

"Barney?—Sally?—the kid?" the teamster demanded, raucously.

"Back—and goin' to live," said Moody. "The Injuns up to Red Shirt heard where the little feller was and was goin' on the war-trail, sudden, but the mother came down on the stage to-day,—and got her pretty little kid."

"Oh, God! I didn't deserve it!" said Slivers, and letting himself fall limply to the earth, he lay with his face in the curve of his arm and shook with emotion.

THE REPARATION

BY EMERY POTTLE

He looked up from the desk where he had been sitting for the last hour, his head down on his arms, trying to shut out the brave, old cry of life coming in through the open windows, pulling gently at his heart, cheeping through the darkened room as lightly and as blithely as the birds in the horse-chestnut tree just outside—the brave cry of life that, somehow, for all its clamorous traditions, seemed just then something peaceful, something that held release, freedom.

He stared about him, furtively, for an instant, as if instinctively on his guard against an unwelcome eye. Then, presently, he smiled, and going to a window, pushed open the blinds, leaning, with elbows on the sill, gratefully out into the rectangular enclosure, walled in high by houses, where the late afternoon sun glanced with uncertain warmth on the horse-chestnut.

There was now, he told himself, no use of evading or denying it longer; right or wrong, things had come to a point with him where anything but the truth was unbearable; it was there, like a live thing with him in the room, and out in the court, too,—almost as if he could put out his hand and draw it in close to him. Freedom, that was it. His lips made the word noiselessly, again and again, fascinated with the sensation. "Free, free," he kept whispering, stretching out his hands greedily, drawing in full breaths of the late September air.

"I'm glad, that's all there is to it—glad. I can't help being glad—I've tried, too, but now, to-day, it's bound to come out. Glad! It's like being let out of school."

That word—school—brought him back sharply. It seemed to precipitate all the old worry in the solution that but a moment ago was so clear. He came back hesitatingly from the window and threw himself down before the desk again, unable to restrain something he vaguely named his conscience from its weary accusations.

"It's an awful thing. It's true, it is. I'm a beast. I'm all wrong to be like this. It's a terrible thing to be glad a person is—" He shivered as he withheld the end of the sentence, though he realized his cowardice in so withholding. "And that person your—" Again he hesitated.

Haldane, by the desk, was a figure to make, involuntarily, demands on one's sympathy. It seemed all his life—perhaps thirty years long—he had been doing this in one way or another, and by no effort of his. People had a fashion of "looking out for him." Not that he had grown up particularly incapable or helpless; it might rather have been due to a certain appealing gentleness of bearing, something that was the resultant of a half-shy manner, expanding into boyish confidence winningly; a shortish, slender figure, scarcely robust; eager, friendly brown eyes behind his glasses; and a keen desire to be liked. It might be seen, in the present sharp nervous play of emotion over his face, how utterly he was unsuited to the weight of mental discomfort,—how it fretted and galled him. That he was a gentleman, and by nature of a morbidly just and fair disposition, only made his present distress the more intolerable to him.

"Lord God," he muttered, hopelessly, "why, *why* had it all to be?" And this question might, in the end, be taken as an aimless appeal to the Almighty to know why He had deliberately led him into a wretchedly miserable condition of mind and left him there.

It was the day after Ida's burial—Haldane's wife's burial. A week ago he had taken her to a city hospital, and she had died there—she and her baby—in the night, away from Haldane. He had gone dazedly, very conscientiously, through the dreadful, relentless activity that follows immediately on the heels of death; there was some alleviation in the thought that everything had been done just as *she* would have liked to have it. To-day the house was free of the grieving, sickening smell of flowers; the last of the people had mercifully fulfilled their duty to Ida and him and had gone, leaving him the humiliation of their honest, warm-hearted words and halting phrases of sympathy.

"Great God!" he had kept saying to himself as he listened to them, "if you *knew*,—if you *knew*!"

At times he felt, as he thought of those friends, secretly resentful. "If it hadn't been for them, I don't believe I," he caught himself saying—"I'd ever have married." But again he stopped his mental train abruptly. It was such a wearisome business, this "being fair"—he put it so—to *her*; this conscientious erasing of self-justification which he felt to be so unworthy. It would have been such a relief to Haldane to be, for an hour, obliviously selfish in his estimate of his two years of marriage with Ida.

There had been nothing, after all, remarkable in Haldane's

experience—save for him; nothing very far removed from the commonplace. His father—a simple-hearted musician—had trained his son in music since the days when the lad could first hold a violin under his little chin. He had died when the boy was twenty, and Haldane had gone on, contentedly enough and absorbed, to take his father's place among the violins of an orchestra, and to teach music. As he grew older his father's friends told him he was leading a wretchedly lonely life; that he ought to marry. And at this Haldane smiled his deprecating, affectionate smile—a smile that, somehow, convinced his advisers in their own wisdom.

When Ida Locke came to live in a hall bedroom of the untidy boarding-house Haldane for years had called home, it was not long before she, too, quite unaffectedly, took to the idea that the good-natured musician needed "looking after." And since, all her life, she had tremendously given herself to the care of people around her, it was no unusual experience—she sought it frankly, importantly.

It is scarcely probable that, in the beginning, any thought of ultimate marriage entered her head. Those who knew her invariably said, "Ida is a sensible girl." Rather, her "looking after" Haldane took itself out in the hearty channels of dry boots, overshoes, tea of late afternoons, candid suggestions as to proper winter underwear, remedies for his frequent colds. This solicitude—which was, in essence, quite maternal—made a bond between the two; this and the fact that they both were workers—for Ida taught English in a private school.

It is hardly necessary to elaborate their romance, if it was such, from this point. Gradually, hastened by the awful propinquity in a third-rate boarding-house, Haldane really came to believe—as along the line of least resistance—in his personal incapacity and his loneliness; gradually Ida Locke began to realize that, for the first time, this Love she had read of and dreamed of doubtfully had become a reality for her. She was not a little amazed and gratified at its plain practicability—its *sensibleness*, she put it.

That she so liked him—indeed, he liked *her* enormously, he considered—assured Haldane in his moments of misgiving. The very largeness in her ample effect of good looks, her genius for managing his affairs and hers, her prim neatness of dress, her utter freedom from any sort of weak dependence on him, her uncompromising rigidity of moral attitude, and, above all, her *goodness* to him—this convinced him of her ultimate fitness to be a wife to him; and it must be said that he had never heretofore given anything but the scantest attention to the matter of sentimental attachments; it had not occurred to him, definitely, that he was even likely some day to fall splendidly in love.

So when he asked her, shyly, gently, to marry him she consented frankly—too frankly, Haldane almost admitted. And since, in the world as she knew it, men did not ask women to marry them unless they loved them really, she took much for granted, and began, at once, to look for a cheap flat.

Ida gave up her teaching when they married and went to their Harlem flat. Indeed, she considered this her domestic right; now, after almost a dozen years—she was older than Haldane—of instruction, she wanted "to rest, and keep house," she told her husband.

Then, suddenly, illogically perhaps, after not more than three months of it, Haldane knew it was all quite intolerable to him. Before the desk to-day, Ida's desk, he saw luminously just how intolerable it had been—these two years of marriage.

The more irritatingly unbearable, too, it was because of the excellence of Ida's qualities—qualities he had taken humorously before marriage, but which later he had to take seriously. He began to hate her constant and intimate possession of his motives and tastes, her inquiries as to what he ate for lunch, and whether he considered his flannels quite adequate. He childishly resented her little nagging economies—and especially because he knew they were generally necessary. He chafed at the practical, sensible view he was argued resolutely into on every matter. What made it hard was that Haldane could not decently account for his revulsion of feeling toward Ida, now she was his wife. Worse than all, he saw how lightly she held in esteem his music—his one real love. To her it was a graceful trade to earn a living by—nothing else. And when she finally made it out that in his position in the orchestra he was likely never to rise much higher, unconsciously the fiddling seemed to her rather more of a small business. She told him he ought to be more ambitious.

One night Haldane had played to Ida—he resented so her name Ida—parts of the score of a light opera he had been at work on for years;—he would never play it on the boarding-house piano.

The moment was as vivid for Haldane now as it was then. He could hear again her brisk cheerful voice when he had finished and was waiting—more hopeful than he had ever yet been with her: "That's *pretty*. It's funny—isn't it, dear?—to think you made it up out of your own head. I never *could* understand—Leonard, have you got entirely rid of your sore throat?—Why don't you try to sell some of your little tunes?"

The disappointment of it all, for an instant, had brought angry tears to his eyes. He remembered now just the bitter hopelessness of feeling how she had failed him—and the remembrance hurt anew. That night he had seen almost clearly how it was to be with him and her in all the years to come.

There was, in Haldane's subsequent attitude toward the question of his marriage to Ida Locke, nothing worth the name of heroic. Indeed, looked at from the commonplace, critical standpoint, the situation was not so bad. It was Haldane's personal conception of it which caused the difficulty. Probably it was his sense of fairness to *her* which made him accept matters quietly—as he did accept them. It was his comfort to-day, out of all the ruck of his artificial self-reproach, that Ida had never known—as he said—how he felt toward her.

"She never knew," he repeated often, "she never knew. She couldn't, I'm sure. Thank God for that!"

What she had never known was, in Haldane's mind, his real idea of her as his wife. For he had been very kind; he had patiently let her look out for him; he had kept the fret of his heart off his tongue, and the sulkiness of his temper off his face. What he had not succeeded in doing, however, was to keep the hurt of his soul out of his eyes. So they had gone on with it for the two years, with a prospect of going on with it forever, Haldane growing daily quieter, more reserved, if anything more gently kind, and more pathetically hopeless. With Ida it was, rather, a large, legitimate outlet for all the sensibleness, practicality, capable qualities, she so generously possessed. It seemed to her, when she knew her child was coming, that she was wonderfully reaching the culmination of womanhood and wifehood. Yet, after all, it had been but just death for Ida.

All this was running through Haldane's brain as he sat, on the day after his wife's burial, before her little oak desk. And the result he had to make out of it was always the same:

"I'm glad it's over. I'm *glad*."

*　*　*　*　*

The room seemed less burdensome when he came back to it late that night. Oppressed with the hatefulness of his attitude of the afternoon, Haldane had seized his hat and had fled out into the streets. He had dined at a restaurant, a thing he had not done in years, and had listened to a bad orchestra play cheerful tunes—tunes that somehow livened him up, stayed comfortably in his mind afterwards. Every one he saw seemed so happy. He assured himself that happiness—a quiet content, at least—was to be *his* now. Why not? Why disguise the fact that he was really, underneath, glad? So he smiled and lingered and sipped his coffee, feeling suddenly the beautiful realization that he was again of the world—irresponsible, careless. Coming back into the dull flat was not half the gloomy effort he had fancied it was going to be. For one blessed thing, he came when he chose. Besides, something had given him a sense of his right, his cheerful right, to be as he liked, what he liked. Haldane went about the tiny rooms humming gently; he played softly on the piano some old love-songs he had composed when he was twenty—things *she* had never heard.

Presently he sat down, lighted a fresh cigarette, and set himself to thinking out matters anew.

"It was a mistake, that's all," he said, at last. "And that's plain. A mistake for me. But now it's all over and done with. There's nothing to be got out of this endless accusing and regret over something that couldn't be helped—helped, at least, after it was once started.... I'll always wear my hurt of it; that I know. It hurts like the devil to think I didn't—

couldn't—give her the love she ought to have had. If there were any way—any possible way of reparation, ... but I suppose there isn't. Nothing except to live decently and honorably—if that's reparation. Thank God, 'tisn't as if there were any other woman mixed up in it—I haven't got that to worry me at any rate. I wonder whether a man gets his punishment for—but no, you can't help feeling, and being, and loving, just as it comes. It's this dreadful unconventionality of—not really liking—loving a person you are supposed to love that warps your judgment. And we lie about it to ourselves and to others till when we have to face the real truth we go all to pieces.... But, just the same, I'd feel so much easier if there *were* only some way I could make it up to Ida now that she's gone. Poor Ida, poor Ida."

Haldane's eyes strayed to the little, cheap desk again, and for a moment the distress of the afternoon was renewed. But he resolutely threw off the accusing mood he so feared. There was a pile of letters lying there—letters that he had had neither the time nor the heart to look into for the past week. He picked them up now with relief at finding something tangible to be done. Most of them were letters of consolation and sympathy for him from his friends and hers; the worn phrases one can so little avoid in such missives touched him with a sense of their dual ineffectuality. Other letters were addressed to Ida—commonplace messages and bills which she had not been able to open. And there was one from her mother—written evidently before she had heard of her daughter's imminent illness and death. This last Haldane laid aside until he had finished the others; and even then he looked at it long and somewhat tenderly before he opened it.

"It must have come very hard to her; Ida was all she had," he considered. "It must have been very hard." He thought of the tear-stained, illegible letter Ida's mother had sent him after she had had his telegram. An illness had prevented her from coming to the funeral; and she lived so far away, somewhere in Iowa. Her heart was bleeding for *him*, she wrote. Her own loss was almost blotted out in the thought of *his* terrible grief. He had never finished it—that letter; he could not. Such words had seemed too sacred for him to read, feeling as he did. So he had torn it up.

"Ida was very good to her mother," he reflected; "at least she was conscientiously always trying to do her best by her, support her and all that. She took it awfully as a duty—but she did it."

Once, after they were married, Ida had gone back, for six months, to the private school that she might have money to send her mother in a sudden financial stress. Haldane thought of that, too, with keen regret that he had not been able to earn the necessary money himself—he was ill that winter. Yes, surely, Ida had been splendid in the matter of her mother. "It's a pity that things weren't so that Ida's mother could have come to see us here in New York," Haldane said, as he opened the envelope—"come before Ida died." The letter itself was not long. When he had finished with it—and this only after a third reading—he laid it down slowly and stared silently at the fine old-fashioned characters.

"Great God!" he said at last, gently, "the poor old lady!"

"My dear daughter," ran the letter, "mother is so sorry to have to tell you this now when all your thoughts and energies must be centred on the wonderful event so soon to happen. It seems to me I've always been calling on you for help and you have done so much. Oh, it hurts me to have to worry and distress you now, dear.

"The truth is that Mr. Liddell is going to foreclose the mortgage on the house. He says he cannot wait longer than a week or two. I've tried every way to get the interest, but I can't do it. The little I had left, your cousin George invested for me, and now he tells me—I don't understand it at all—that it's quite lost. I know you'll say I was foolish to let George have it, but he promised so much—and George has been so good to me. I won't ask you and Leonard to give me a home; that would be unfair to you both. I'm so distressed and upset. Write me, if you can, and tell me what you think is best." And there was more in the same distressed key.

Haldane was as near his decision, perhaps, when he laid down the letter as hours afterward when he stumbled to bed. It was strangely clear to him—the attitude he was to assume. Not that he did not make a fight of it, and a sharp fight. But, after all, he knew from the first how it was destined to end.

"I asked for my chance to make it up to her," he muttered. "Well, I've got it, haven't I? Isn't this it? If where *she* is she knows to-night that I never loved her—sometimes even hated her—then she knows that I'll try to pay it back to her in the only way I can. I'll bring her mother here to live with me.... My God! and I wanted so the *freedom* of it all again, just to feel *free*.... No, this is it—my way—I'll take it. It's what I owe Ida. I can't reason it out logically and I dare say the world would put it straight that I didn't have to do this—take her mother—but I will. I wouldn't feel right about it in this life or in any next if I didn't. Yes, that's the reparation."

Haldane's last thought before he slept that night, as it was in the fortnight before she came, was, "What is Ida's mother like? I wonder if—she is like—like Ida?"

*   *   *   *   *

It had been six months—a whole winter and more—since Ida's mother had come to live with Leonard Haldane. And altogether unexpectedly it had been, for Haldane, quite the most beautiful winter he had ever spent. As for Ida's mother—well, when she was alone her eyes were constantly filling with tears—tears of thankfulness that the Lord had sent her, in the language of her frequent prayers of gratitude, a son to stay the declining years of her life—a son to her who had so wanted a son all these years.

Haldane could never forget that night he had gone, with sharp misgivings, to the station to meet Mrs. Locke. "I suppose I'm a fool," he had muttered, as he paced miserably up and down the draughty, smoky enclosure where her train, already very late, was to come in. "But it's my debt to the dead I'm going to pay." He added a moment later: "What I shall hate most of all, what will be hardest to bear, will be her endless sympathy. For she won't know—she'll never know—just how it was between Ida and me."

He was to look for a "little dried-up, frightened woman in a black bonnet, with a handkerchief in her left hand"—so Mrs. Locke had written him. Haldane had smiled at the frank characterization—that, somehow, didn't sound like Ida's spirit in her mother.

She was the last to come out through the iron gate. Almost he had given her up, she had delayed so long. A little, dried-up, frightened woman in a black bonnet—that was she. Like a tiny, stray cloud, very nervous and out of place. Her face was white with fatigue, the excitement of the journey, and the thought of how she should meet—ought she to call him Leonard? And when Haldane saw her he suddenly smiled boyishly—as if there could be such a thing as a problem over this scared, half-tearful, ridiculously pathetic, white-haired old woman with a black-bordered handkerchief in her shaking left hand.

Before he considered it he had said gently, "Well, mother—"

The tears in her eyes welled over as she gasped in a whisper, "My boy!"

So, after all, there was no awkward, conscious period of adjustment for the two. They took up their life simply and quite as if it were no new thing to them both—as if they had come together again after a long separation. And it was, perhaps, in a way, just that—a coming together of elements that had long been kept apart. "She's not like Ida," Haldane kept saying to himself.

"You're just like a mother in a storybook; the kind you always want when you read about them," Haldane often told her. "You know, I never had one—one that I remember; mine died so long ago."

"And you—you're—quite my son," she would answer shyly, her voice trembling with the joy of it. It was such a regret to her that she hadn't Leonard's readiness of speech and the courage to break down her reserve—for she wanted to tell him, as she said to herself, just how she felt, just how good he was to her.

So it was a beautiful winter for them both. Naturally there was the fact of Ida that had to be faced. That was tremendously hard at first. He constantly felt her grieving for him, for the failure of all his hopes, the wreck of all a man holds so precious. And there were all the details of Ida's sickness and death to be gone over with her mother—the things she had done just before. How she looked; the quantity of flowers; even what she wore for her burial. Instinctively Haldane knew how dear these matters were to her, and he went over them faithfully, effacing his own bitterness of memory as best he might. When Mrs. Locke hesitatingly asked him one evening if—if Ida had—had *said* anything—left any message for *her*, Haldane's heart ached for her; Ida had left no message. He softened it as best he might.

"You see, she didn't know, couldn't know, that—that she was going to die. It was all so sudden, you know, so awfully sudden."

Mrs. Locke nodded. "Yes—I see. Poor Ida! She did so much for me always."

After a month or so, quite unconsciously, they ceased to mention Ida. Haldane, when he thought of it at all—and that with relief—wondered vaguely why Ida's mother did not talk more about her. "Perhaps it's because she doesn't want to keep hurting me," he thought it out, "bless her!"

Gradually the intimacy between Haldane and his mother—for she was quite that to him—grew into a relation that was as rare as it was tender. They both felt it keenly. Their talk was all of him, his affairs, his music. He played to her for hours in the evenings he was not at the orchestra; when he was teaching in the mornings she would steal into the room, and sit, sewing, in a corner, listening gratefully to the dreary routine of his pupils' exercises. She seemed never to tire of "being near Leonard." And always she was asking, "Won't you play a little from *the opera*, Leonard?"

Once she said to him, with her timid smile: "It's like heaven, having so much music all the time. Seems as if all my life I've been just starved to death for tunes."

Haldane bent and kissed her white hair. "Well, mother," he laughed, "it's quite a real piece of heaven to have you around the place."

"You're spoiling me," she cried; "how can I ever go back to Iowa?"

"Who said Iowa in this house?" he demanded of her. "You're to stay always—as long as you can stand me—*always*."

"My son!" she kept murmuring after he had gone, as if she loved the words on her lips. "He's just the kind of son I used to hope I might have," she sighed. "I don't see—it's so strange why he's so good to me. I'm not at all like *her*. Ida was so sensible always, and I'm not at all—Ida always told me I couldn't take care of myself, that I was very foolish. I don't see why Leonard is so kind to me. It must he just because I'm her mother. Leonard must have loved her so much, and understood her. Poor Ida!"

*   *   *   *   *

The spring had broken through its first slender greenish film into the freshness of its young beauty. The sense of faint, far voices endlessly calling was in the air. Again the windows of the little flat were opened and again the afternoon sun warmed to golden green the new growth of leaves on the horse-chestnut in the rectangular enclosure outside.

Haldane had never felt so splendidly the birth of new things—in himself and in the world. All the morning he had been constantly picking up his violin, playing what he called his "Spring-feelings"—unrhythmic wild snatches of melody.

"God! it's good, good, *good*," he cried, throwing back his head. "Good to have lived out of it all into this."

"Mother," he called presently, "what on earth are you doing there all alone? Come out and play with me. You've looked over those old books and papers, spring-cleaned your old closets, too long. If you don't come out at once, I'll come and drag you out bodily—I will indeed."

He ran to her door in another moment, and flinging it open wide, he called: "If you will insist on being led forth—Why, mother, what is it? what's the matter? *What is it? Are you ill?* Why—"

She sat on a low stool drawn up close to her bed. Her hands were clasped straight out before her over a little book bound in faded imitation red leather—a little book Haldane, on the instant, with curious alertness, knew as one of Ida's old school note-books. On her face was a look so bewildered, so grieved, so terror-stricken almost, that Haldane suddenly ceased to speak. She raised her eyes to him with the pleading of a hurt animal. For a time neither uttered a word. And then, all at once, it seemed to Haldane as if he *knew*. His gaze fell hesitatingly. When, at last, he spoke, it was in a very gentle voice.

"Mother—is it anything we can talk out together—now?"

She shook her head dumbly, the tears gathering in her eyes. "Oh, Lennie!" she whispered, finally, as if he were a little boy. "It isn't true, is it?"

Haldane did not reply. She reached out the little red book to him slowly. "You'd—you'd better read it. I—found it—this afternoon."

He took the book, without wonder, and went back, softly closing the door on her. Unconsciously he sat down before the little, cheap, oak desk—Ida's desk—and began to read. It was, perhaps, two hours afterward when he had finished. The room was dark and very still.

"So she knew," he said, slowly. "After all, she knew. And I never guessed." His head sank down on his arms.

It was a curious inconsistency in the mind of Ida Locke which had prompted her to write in that red-covered note-book just what she had written. No one would have guessed the secret strain of introspection in her, nor guessed the impulse which led her to put into writing her hidden life. Unless, indeed, that introspection and that impulse are always part of the intuitions of love—yielded to or not, as may be. The entries were scattered—as if put down when the stress of feeling had overcome her. They ranged over the two years of their married life. In each one she had seemed, with a startling lucidity, to have apprehended exactly her husband's state of mind toward her. She had written freely, baldly, without excess of sentimentality. "I know he hates me sometimes; I see it in his eyes." Again: "He is hideously kind." "He lives in a mental room that I can't break into." In another place it ran: "Why is it? I am his mental equal; his superior in education. I'm his wife and he asked me to marry him. And yet he can't bear to have me near him. He hates me to-day." "I'm afraid," she wrote again, "how Leonard will regard our child. If he should hate it, too. Perhaps we shall both not live through it." And so it ran on, with awful candor.

"I'm so sorry she had to know," Haldane sighed again and again. "And, now, what's to be the end of it? What will Ida's mother do? Lord God, she'll never forgive me—never."

*　*　*　*　*

Late that night Mrs. Locke came in. Haldane had scarcely stirred from his chair. The note-book lay open before him on the desk. He looked at her compassionately, for now his thoughts were all for the shrinking, hurt woman beside him. She had never before seemed so fragile, so dependent, and yet he could not but mark in her hearing a new resolution of forces, a dignity as of a stern decision. Haldane did not wait for her to question.

"You will want to know," he began, wearily, "if all this written here is true. All this Ida wrote down. You want to ask me that? It's—it's all true, quite true." He waited, but she gave no sign. "Quite true; I—I suppose it wouldn't be worth while for me to explain things now. You will think I've lied to you all along. In a way, I have. No, I suppose you don't want to hear me make futile explanations, excuses."

"If there—there is anything to be said, Leonard, you had better say it—now," she answered, nervously, twisting her handkerchief in her fingers.

He hesitated painfully. "Everything I might say seems to be trying to shift the load from my shoulders on to—another's," he said, at last. "It was a mistake—that's all. A mistake for us. Before it began—our marriage—it was different, but afterward—She was very good to me; looked after me and all that, but—Oh, I'm afraid I'm only hurting you the worse by saying all this. You won't, you can't understand. Let it be that it was all my fault. It was, it was. Believe that, please.... And I know you won't want to stay here with me any longer—after this. I quite understand that. A man who—who felt as she wrote it all down here—such a man you wouldn't, you couldn't—" He stopped hopelessly. "I can't bear to have you go," he burst out, impulsively. "Where will you go? Back there to Iowa?"

She nodded sorrowfully.

"And have no more music? And—and—oh, it's cruel. *Why* had you to find it out? It didn't matter anyway when it was all done with. Why *did* you have to know? ... And you haven't any money. You must let me help you. Let me do that—just that. Can't you forget it all enough for that? Surely you've liked me—for what you've liked in me, let me help you. Great heavens, if I thought of you alone out there, without money—*Must* you go?"

Haldane was fast losing control of himself. With an effort he pulled himself together and tried to smile.

"You're right to go," he said. "Right. You wouldn't want anything to do with me now."

He looked up at her, though loath to meet her eyes. There was a wonderful pity in her face. "Don't!" he cried, sharply, not understanding.

"I want to say this," he broke out again, almost roughly. "I never guessed that she knew how I felt toward her. I wasn't cruel or beastly—I was kind. They say that's cruelty, too. I tried—my God! how I tried!—never to let her know the truth. That's all I can say for myself; ... you'd better go."

She was so silent that at last he faced her again. She was crying softly, and, it appeared, without bitterness. Haldane stared at her curiously.

"I wanted to know that—that last you said," Mrs. Locke gasped, with difficulty. "I—I—I've been thinking it all over in my room. It's very hard to say—please let me go on with it just as I can, I—I've said I wanted to hear that last. But I knew it—in my heart—all the time. I knew you couldn't be cruel to a living thing. And—and—somehow—it changed—things. I've had such a terrible struggle all alone. I've tried to pray over it and—oh, I'm afraid I'm very wrong and very wicked—I almost know I am." Her voice sank to a whisper. "But—oh, Leonard ... somehow I just seemed to feel inside me just how you felt, just how—it was with you those two years. Oh, it's a dreadful thing to say, isn't it? Poor Ida! She was so good to me, and yet sometimes—" The trembling old woman's voice faltered and broke.

Haldane's eyes were full of tears. A great light was slowly breaking for him. He dared not speak.

"Don't think I'm a wicked old woman, Leonard; I never even guessed—till I came here—how I felt. And then you were like a son—my son—the boy I wanted so, and—I loved the music so, and being with you, more than anything I ever knew—it doesn't seem as if—"

Haldane put his hand on hers gently, "As if you could go away now?"

She turned to him with a little sad smile, and in her face was a sweet dignity.

"Yes, I cannot go—now, my son."

THE YEARLY TRIBUTE

BY ROSINA HUBLEY EMMET

"For science is a cruel mistress. She exacts a yearly tribute of flesh and blood like the dragons of ancient pagan mythology."

The eminent scientist paused momentarily here and viewed the earnest young faces before him. In this poetic figure of speech he saw fit to present to them the hardships of the life they had chosen to embark upon. It was a hot June morning, and the heavy scent of syringa came in through the high uncurtained windows of the lecture-hall. All the students stared with reverence at this distinguished stranger, who had come a long distance to speak to the graduating class; and one of its members sighed deeply and turned his eyes to the window, and watched some maple leaves moving languidly against the blue sky. The lecturer heard his sigh, saw him fall into abstraction, realized the peculiar character of his face; and marked him as a man who would serve to the end, possibly becoming one of the victims of that cruel mistress.

*   *   *   *   *

Pilchard and Swan had stopped to rest in the middle of the plaza. The black Mexican night was falling and a few stars blossomed in the sky, but there was no abatement in the heat which had held since sunrise; rather, indeed, the thickness of the atmosphere seemed intensified. The two Americans, who had spent a whole year in Mexico and become accustomed to the climate, attempted to make themselves comfortable. Pilchard sank to a dilapidated bench and lighted a cigarette; and Swan, not having even sufficient spirit to smoke, stretched himself bodily on the flat stones which paved the plaza, and placed his old hat upon his upturned face.

Both young men seemed depressed, and without speaking they listened to the moaning of the ocean which heaved and glistened in the distance; and when Pilchard finally said, "So poor Murphy is gone too," and Swan responded, "His troubles are over, poor fellow," it showed how completely they had been absorbed in the same thought.

"And Mulligan last week," Pilchard continued, "and all the others who went before, and Peele taken sick this afternoon. Swan, we're the only white men left."

"And we've only got ten days left."

"Oh, I guess we can do it, so long as we're out of the swamp."

"So long as the swamp isn't in us."

They were alluding to the railroad they had come to Mexico to build. The time-limit given in the contract would expire in ten days, and it would be a race to get the tracks through the town and down to the new docks in that time. Swan, whenever he thought of it, became restless, and now he sat up with a jerk, and his old hat slipped off his face. Even in that dim light Swan's ugliness was apparent. He measured over six feet and was loose-jointed and ungainly; he had big flat feet, and big bony, capable hands; and his features, which were big and bony too, seemed in proportion to nothing but his general ungainliness. Swan was an inventive Yankee with no background and no tradition. He could not even claim the proverbial Connecticut farm. His people had been dreary commercials in a middle-sized New Hampshire town, and he had worked his way through college to fit himself for a scientific career. His memory of his deceased parents was so colorless that it seemed to Swan as if they had never existed, and his contacts had been so dull, his outlook so dreary, that he had almost no conception of beauty. His plain college room, where, by the hour, he had worked out mathematical problems, and a grimy engine-room (which was the next stage of his advancement), where he had stood in a greasy black shirt, surrounded by an unceasing whir of machinery, and bossed a gang of men—these had been the things which had substituted for him romance and passion and life; and finally, when Pilchard, a college friend, had persuaded him to come down to Mexico and build a railroad, he had taken off his greasy black shirt and gone, principally because this was such a big undertaking, and it would undoubtedly in the end lead to something very much bigger.

The company which was causing the railroad to be built had established large exporting-houses in San Francisco, which sent down certain articles of merchandise to Mexico, and the railroad was designed to transport this freight from one of the southwestern seaport towns to the city of Mexico. The undertaking included the erection of docks with swinging elevators to lift the freight from the vessels and deposit it in the cars, and as the pay was very large and Pilchard was an adventurous soul, he undertook the job when it was offered to him, and going to the manager's office, impressed him with his boldness and ability, and signed his name to the contracts without reading them through; then gayly, and feeling no uneasiness, he buttoned his coat over the neatly folded paper and went to see Swan.

Swan, in a greasy black shirt, was in the engine-room, hard at work, and he was just about to reprimand one of the men when Pilchard came in. Although it was early in May, a spell of precocious heat had taken New York by the throat, and what with the whir of rapidly turning wheels, and the smell of hot machine-oil and perspiring men, there was something filthy and degraded about the atmosphere. Swan suddenly realized this, although it was the only atmosphere he knew anything about. Glancing upward, he saw a little patch of blue sky through the top of one of the grimy windows ... a white cloud sailed past ... and then another ... something akin to longing welled in his heart, something like a wave of despair and hope, a desire to lift himself into a higher and less degraded world.... He looked toward the door and saw Pilchard, and crossing the room, he greeted him warmly and read the contract Pilchard pulled from his pocket.

"That's a queer business," said Swan, when he had finished.

"How so?"

"Man alive, haven't you read what you've signed your name to?"

"Certainly I've read it."

"And you think you can put the job through in a year?"

"Why not?" asked Pilchard, with his "cock-sure" smile.

Swan, like every one else, was taken in by this smile, and to convince himself he read the contract again, out loud this time, and in a thoughtful way. Pilchard listened.

The contract guaranteed that a railroad covering two hundred and fifty miles, between the city of Mexico and the little seaport of Zacatula, on the Pacific Ocean, would be built and completed in one year's time, work starting on the 25th of June. Docks and freight-elevators were included in the work, and if the tracks were not in fit condition for the trains to run by the date specified, every penny of the very large pay would be forfeited by the builders. A strange contract, indeed! Pilchard, however, as he heard it read, betrayed by no sign that he was as much surprised as Swan.

"Well," said Swan, looking up and meeting that "cock-sure" smile, "you think you can do it in a year?"

"I'm certain I can."

"Of course," Swan continued, not yet convinced, "it's the worst country on earth; full of swamp and yellow fever."

"I'll run in a gang of Mexican Indians to lay the ties. They can stand their own climate."

"But you'll have to take down some white men, too, good fellows who know the business. You can't be the only man to do the bossing. It'd kill you."

All this time Pilchard was closely watching Swan, and almost unconsciously something had been growing in his mind. Swan had an ugly, resolute face, and endurance seemed to be expressed in every line of his body. Behind him the engine roared, and spit steam, and ground out the produce of a great city factory; his face and hands were grimy and covered with grease, and the black cinders around his deep-set eyes gave him a terrible, deathly look. Pilchard saw instantly that he must have Swan to do the work. He must take him down to Mexico or else the railroad would never be built. Swan would come, too, because there was a look of tragic fatigue in his deep-set eyes, an expression of sick nausea in the lines about his mouth, that showed how gladly he would change, how completely he had come to the end of his hopes here; so Pilchard suggested with a careless smile that they go down to Mexico together. "Of course," he said, "I don't say that it mightn't be better for me to do it alone—two heads to a job, you know, isn't always a good arrangement; but you've got a pretty mean berth here. It'll take years for you to get a rise, and you're wasting your youth and health shut up with this filthy gang of men. This job of mine would push you right along, and you'll get others like it. Better come."

Swan reflected. His work was the only thing on earth that he cared for, and to progress in his work, to keep putting through more and more difficult jobs, was what he had always aimed to do. But had he a right to take advantage of Pilchard's generosity? He glanced around the room, conscious of the incessant chattering of the different parts of the engine, which he must keep going in order to turn out the produce of a great city factory. He was no more here than one of the many parts of that engine, and if some day he should be absorbed into the midst of those whirring wheels and ground up like corn, who would ever be the wiser?

So he went.

* * * * *

"Had a letter from the company today," Pilchard observed, suddenly.

"That so?"

"They're going to send a fellow down from Frisco on the

steamer that touches on the 25th. Everything plays into their hands. Steamer reaches here the day the contract expires."

"Well, that's all right."

"They request that I meet the fellow and show him around."

"That's easy, too."

Pilchard breathed smoke through his nose in his self-possessed way, and said nothing more, until Swan suddenly broke out:

"Well, I for one won't be sorry to get out of this hole. I'll get the job done, of course, but we've just had a terrible setback. I think Peele's dying."

"Lord!"

"I came away from him only half an hour ago. He may last through the night, but I doubt it. Anyhow, if he lives or dies, we're devilish pressed for time. I'm beginning to think we'll have to work at night, too."

"At night?"

"There's a full moon. Here she comes now." Swan looked at the full moon, which, as the darkness increased, grew in radiance.

Pilchard breathed more smoke through his nose, then said with a sigh: "That's hard luck, Swan. I'm sorry."

"Hey?"

"And yet it's a lucky thing that you're as strong as you are.

It's a lucky thing you haven't got the responsibilities at home that I have."

"I don't see what you mean."

"Why, you know I'm engaged! I'm as good as married. That poor girl's got everything ready for the wedding. You met her that day last year you came up to Maine before we left New York."

"Yes, I met her."

"And you remember how much she thought of me?" Pilchard spoke slowly. It was impossible to tell why he did so. Was it because he did not care to discuss the woman he loved with an outsider like Swan, or was it because he was going on tiptoe, because he wondered what he must say next, because he was waiting, hoping that something unexpected would develop?

Swan, however, dropped the question of Pilchard's marriage.

"You mean, I suppose, that you won't work at night."

"I can't. I'm not well enough."

Swan grunted and sighed and stretched all his limbs, shaking his great shoulders as if he were trying to shake out the ague. Then he cleared his throat again and turned to Pilchard.

"See here, Pilchard, it's time we came to some understanding."

"Understanding?" Pilchard queried in a surprised voice.

"Yes, about this job. About the pay—m—not so much the

pay as the credit. This job ought to give a man a name. It's been a big piece of engineering and devilish hard work to put it through. I've planned the whole thing and watched every stroke of what's been done, and I deserve at least half the credit, if not all."

Swan spoke in a brutal, masterful way. Perhaps he realized as he did so how completely the acknowledgment of his services depended on Pilchard's generosity. Pilchard alone had signed the contract, and Swan's existence was no more to the company than the existence of the other workmen. Moreover, the eleven mechanics they had brought down had all been carried off by fever, and there was no one else who, in case of necessity, could testify to the splendid work Swan had done, practically alone. All this was in Pilchard's mind as well as Swan's, and all this suddenly showed Pilchard how completely Swan was in his power. He must play a careful game.

"Why, what the devil do you mean?" he asked, speaking rather angrily.

"What do I mean? I mean that this is all too unbusinesslike. It's too vague. I'm risking my life to put this business through, and I want to get what I deserve. It's the biggest thing I've ever done, and I won't do it for nothing."

"For nothing? Man alive, you're almost accusing me of dishonesty! I told you when we started out that I'd give you half the pay. If I'd ever supposed you didn't trust my word I'd have had it drawn up on paper. And as for the credit, you deserve it all, and you'll get it all ... and that's all."

Pilchard ended with a self-conscious laugh, and got up to go indoors and take a few drinks before he went to bed. He stood for a moment, uncertainly, before Swan, wondering with a strange distrust, which lately had been growing upon him, what Swan really thought. Swan was so silent and reserved, and he worked with such unflinching constancy, that Pilchard often felt as if he too must be developing some plan. It was fortunate, he told himself, that there were only ten days more. His nerves could not have held out much longer; but after he had filled himself with several drinks and was sitting in gauzy pajamas beside an open window, things began to look brighter. Ten days might develop unheard-of things. To work all night on the borders of a swamp in this rainy season, which is almost certain death for a white man—Pilchard closed his eyes and peacefully slept....

Swan continued to sit on the bench, and throwing back his head, looked at the sky. A full moon swung above him, huge and tropical and red, seeming to garnish the black depths that lay behind it and that great black mouth that opened immeasurably into the west. All his actual surroundings faded away, and, as is often the case with men at these moments, he thought of a woman that he had seen once and had never forgotten.

That cool summer day just a year ago that he had spent on the coast of Maine, whither he had gone to see Pilchard about some final arrangements for their journey to Mexico—Pilchard had introduced him to the girl he was going to marry, and it had somehow happened that he and she had taken a short walk together along a cliff where some pines were growing, and which looked forlornly enough across the solitary ocean. Nothing but the most commonplace words had passed between them; they had talked of Pilchard and his enterprise, and had stopped to look at the view, and had gazed out over the rolling waves. He had scarcely dared look at his companion, but once he had helped her over some rocks, and he remembered that her foot had slipped, and for an instant her body had swayed against his. He remembered, too, that she had pale cheeks and dreamy eyes, and a slim hand laden with rings that held back her skirts. This slight experience had made a changed man of him. New senses existed for him, new hopes for the future that turned him dizzy, a splendid and deeper insight into life. The sordid realities of his life no longer claimed all his thoughts; they were beautified by rare and exquisite dreams, and by repetitions of that strange welling of hope and despair which had come to him in the grimy engine-room. After all, there were things in the world other than engines and boilers and steel tracks; there were plenty of uses for him besides calculating and experimenting and bossing a lot of filthy men. He, too, could serve and wait and hope and ... die!

*　　*　　*　　*　　*

Swan spent the remainder of that night with Peele, and as the sick man was still alive at sunrise, and Swan was obliged to oversee the men, he swallowed some coffee and went off, leaving Pilchard in charge. About noon Pilchard came out to him with a white face.

"What's the matter?" Swan asked, full of apprehension.

"Peele died before you'd been gone an hour."

"We must see to having him buried at once."

"He's underground already."

"Where we'll all be if we stay much longer."

"Where I feel as if I ought to be," Pilchard groaned.

"What d'ye mean?"

"I mean that I'm about ready to give up. If it wasn't for you I would give up. I'm as weak as water. I just saw Peele die, and that finished me. Ugh! It was awful!"

And Pilchard, who certainly was pale, drew a flask from his pocket and took a long drink. He seemed to drink to his own weakness. He seemed to glory in the fact that he had given up, and that he knew Swan never would.

Swan realized this and looked wearily across the swamp they had just covered. It was all his work. A narrow mound of solid earth ran back as far as eye could reach, and on it two shining steel rails glittered in the blazing sun. On either side lay wet, poisonous ground covered with deadly growths and exuding fearful odors and devitalizing forces which even the heat could not dissipate. In that noonday light which burned and burned and made no impression on the moisture, Swan's face was wilted like a white flower which is dead and turning yellow. His eyes, too, were like things once living and now dead. The muscles around his mouth twitched like electric wire.

"It isn't possible for me to finish it alone," he told himself. He knew that he could finish the job by working both night and day, but could he stand the strain? Had he, after all, a stronger physique than any other white man had ever had before? He leaned far back as if he were trying to fold himself up, and then bent forward in the same manner, trying, with a desperation like death, to relieve the weakness that was numbing his limbs. He suddenly felt dizzy as he looked at the hot distance where some big leaves were waving—dizzy as he knew that he must fail.

"By God!" he exclaimed, striking the pile of dirt. "By God! I'll do it!"

Pilchard put on his hat and smiled. He had been waiting for this. "If you say you will, I bet you will!" he told Swan. "That's why you'll always come out ahead." As he said this he looked intently at Swan, who was still sitting on the pile of dirt. He noticed for the first time the peculiar look in his eyes and the trembling of his whole body.

Swan sat silent. He saw the dark perspiring bodies of the Indians who were laying ties, and his lifelong ambition to be a great engineer suddenly presented itself to him in the old strong unemotional way.

"For science is a cruel mistress. She exacts her yearly tribute of flesh and blood like the dragons of ancient pagan mythology."

This had been said by an eminent scientist who had addressed his graduating class. Swan had heard it then and remembered it now. He clearly remembered that hot June morning ten years ago. Some young maple leaves had made a lovely pattern on the blue northern sky outside the uncurtained windows of the lecture-hall. He remembered that he had looked through the window and vowed that he would never give up.

He organized two bands of men, one to work by moonlight and one by sunlight; but it was necessary for him to overlook them both, day and night, so it happened that there were just two hours in the twenty-four when he could find any rest. This was when the daily tropical storm broke, late in the afternoon, and all the workmen scampered for shelter. Swan crawled into a shanty the men had put up to hold their tools, and wrapping himself in a blanket, slept until the storm was over. That is to say, for three or four times he slept, but gradually he found it impossible to get any rest, and nobody knew the agonies he endured fighting off the fever, which he felt had marked him for its own. He never looked forward longer than twelve hours, thinking always that the next day would decide his fate, and the next day never did. "If I can keep it off till to-morrow, I guess it won't come back," he repeated, mechanically, standing in the moonlight and dosing himself and bossing the men. But in the morning there was never any abatement in those deadly symptoms which told him that the period of incubation would soon be over; and it almost seemed to him as if his cruel mistress was saving him in some miraculous way to complete her work, for it was not until the evening of the ninth day, when the railroad was finished and the last man paid off, that his temperature rose to fever-heat, his pulse quickened, and his tongue became congested, and this demon of the tropical swamp claimed him for its own.

Early on the morning of the 25th, a Pacific mail-steamer touched at the little port of Zacatula, and a man was put off who came down from San Francisco to do business for the company in the event of the railroad not being completed. He was greatly astonished when Pilchard showed him that the last day's work had been done.

"Then," said the agent, mopping his perspiring bald head, "we may say that you've carried out the contract to the letter, to the very minute. You say you only paid off the men last night?"

"Yes," answered Pilchard, with his engaging smile, and casting a possessive glance down the front of his white trousers. "And it was an awful rush to get the job done." But in spite of Pilchard's sleek figure and social smile, he looked pale that morning. The hot sunlight that bathed the end of the dock met no responsive glow in his cheeks.

The agent hung his handkerchief over the top of a post to dry it, and looked more closely at his companion. "Anything the matter?" he asked, kindly. "You certainly haven't lost anything on the job?"

"No—no." Pilchard brought out that ever-ready smile that was so delightful. "But it's about time to go home. This is a terrible climate. We've lost every white man that came down, eleven all told, except myself and—and—one other, who's dying over in that shed now. Maybe—maybe—he's dead—" Pilchard jerked with his thumb towards a shanty just where the docks joined the land....

*   *   *   *   *

In this rude shanty, knocked together by the workmen to hold their tools, on a heap of sacks and blankets, Swan lay as he had dropped the night before. Pilchard had found him there, and the full moon coming in at the wide opening had revealed a fearful sight—Swan in the throes of terrific fever, his face scarlet, his eyes ferrety and congested, and his swollen tongue lolling between his lips. When he saw Pilchard he asked in a strange voice for water. Pilchard brought him some and felt his forehead. It seemed on fire.

"Pilchard," began Swan, in a deliberate voice, as if he were trying to fight off the delirium, "the swamp got into me, after all. I've taken the fever."

Pilchard, appalled by the terrible sight before him, and the things it suggested, which he could not help but see, leaned against the rude wall, and for once his self-possession deserted him. "Swan," he faltered, "Swan—for God's sake—"

"Hush," Swan interposed, in that same deliberate voice. "Don't lose your head. I'm keeping mine. Am I talking sense?"

"Yes, yes, Swan. Perfectly correctly."

"Then I'll tell you what to do." Swan spoke more and more slowly as the fire mounted to his brain and besieged it. "There's every symptom of fever. You can't deny that."

"Symptoms, Swan? I don't see any. You're worn out, poor fellow. That's all."

"Then what's this?" Swan opened his mouth and showed his scarlet tongue. "And this?" He tore open the breast of his shirt and showed the congested condition of his skin. "But I'll fight death as I fought the fever! I'm not going to die. There's too much for me to do in the world! I'll be a great engineer. I'll make her proud. I vowed it when we looked out over the waves and I wanted to take her in my arms. See here!" and suddenly seizing a pickaxe from the ground beside him, he swung it around his head and sent it whizzing past Pilchard's ear, out through the opening of the shanty. "I've got my muscle and I've got my brain and I'll keep my life. I deserve to live. I deserve it as payment for putting the job through. I'll keep my wife here, too, here in the engine-room, with the pines behind us, and I can look after the men then. Who's that leaning against the wall? Pilchard? Poor fool! Why did you boast you were the only man who had ever loved a woman?"

"Me boast! Heaven forbid," faltered Pilchard.

"Then," shouted Swan, suddenly sitting up and striking out with both arms, "take these things away. All these little black things that are pouring over me. It's a regular shower. It must be a whole city. No! No! They're sparks! They're fire! They burn! They burn! Take the wheels away from me! They're grinding me like corn—oh, Lord! it's heavy, it's heavy! There, there! It crushes me! Now, now it's over. This is—

death—" And he sank back, oppressed by a sudden, and overwhelming load of oblivion.

Swan grew worse toward morning, and though the disease had only attacked him at sunset the night before, so rapid and terrible were its onslaughts that by the time the sun rose a complete physical collapse had occurred. His pulse had fallen below normal, and his skin assumed a strange yellow hue, the color of a lemon, and in these signs and the constant hiccough which convulsed the death-stricken frame Pilchard guessed properly what the termination must be. The end would come easily. Swan had ceased to suffer.

When light crept gray and silent into the shanty, Pilchard stood and looked at Swan's prostrate form. No sound came to them but the gentle lapping of the waves. Sober as a dove Day hovered in the sky, and that solemn change which is Death was somewhere near, hiding and waiting; and Pilchard and Death and the breaking Day were for one second alone. And Pilchard was overwhelmed with terror. Some spectre had seized him, and he could not shake it off. He looked once more at the dying man, at his closed eyes and his still body, momentarily convulsed by the final signs of life, like a great piece of machinery when the steam power is gradually running down. Then he turned and broke away, to take a bath and to take a drink and then go to meet the steamer from San Francisco....

*   *   *   *   *

"Eleven? You don't say. Fever, I suppose?"

"Yes. We tackled three swamps on our way down from Mexico."

"That so? Well, it's worth some sacrifice. It's a good job. I wouldn't 'a' undertaken it myself."

"I wouldn't do it again."

They walked down the dock....

Swan opened his eyes and looked through the wide opening
of the shanty out to where the blazing sun struck the hot
water of the little harbor. He hardly remembered where he
was. Oh yes! He must get up and go down-town. In a minute,
when he was fully awake. And he closed his eyes again and
heard the accustomed whir of machinery, and knew that he
was in the engine-room. One of the workmen needed to be
spoken to; he was the filthiest of the lot, and Swan was the
only man who could control him. Suddenly Swan opened his
eyes again and saw that this same workman had entered the
shanty and was standing beside him. He instantly recognized
the man's greasy black shirt.

"For science is a cruel mistress," the man said. "She exacts
her yearly tribute of flesh and blood."

But, singularly enough, these words meant something
entirely different. Swan looked curiously at the workman and
saw that he too was really somebody else. The man smiled
and, leaning over, gently raised him up, and for the first time
in his life Swan felt himself encircled by a woman's arms,
and he tasted a strange, delicious joy awakening deep within
him that knowledge of reciprocal love which slumbers in the
heart of every man.

"And you did it all for me," she said.

"Did what?" he asked her.

"Built the road?"

"Yes," he whispered, closing his eyes again, filled with this new strange joy.

"And now we'll go home together to the North, where the maple leaves make a lovely pattern against the blue sky."

He knew nothing for a minute, and then she spoke again:

"Well, it's a good job. I'll see that you get pushed along. The company 'll have plenty more work; big pay, too. This business has made your name. You're a wonderful fellow! You say you worked night as well as day?"

"For eight days, yes."

It was Pilchard's voice. He was talking to another man. They were leaning heavily against the rough wall of Swan's shanty. A horrible sensation came over the sick man, that sensation experienced by men who emerge from some unnatural mental condition, who are recalled by one sentence, often by one word, which acts like a key and opens again to their terrified vision the horrible realities of actual life. Swan raised his arms to bring that woman's face close to his, but he could not find it. He opened his eyes, and tears of weakness watered his cheeks. He was alone in the hovel knocked together by the men to hold their tools, and the work for which he had given his life was being claimed outside by another man....

The agent leaned against the side of the shanty, gazing reflectively at his steamer, which was anchored half a mile from shore. "I'm going clear round to New York. You'd better get aboard and come with me," he proposed to Pilchard, to whom he had taken a fancy. "Good Lord!" he suddenly shouted, leaping forward. "Is this the shed where you said a workman was dying of fever? Let's get out quick or we'll take the infection."

But Pilchard, pale as death, put up a warning hand. "Yes, let's clear out—let's get to sea before I go crazy! But—but—don't speak so loud. *He may hear!*"

He had heard every word. His faculties, numb with death, sprang instantly into life. He leaped to his feet and left the shanty, momentarily endowed with his full strength, and facing the two men, spoke three times: "My work! My work! My work!" His eyes were on Pilchard all the time, and that look pierced like a sword; it penetrated to the very foundations of his being....

* * * * *

Pilchard caught the body as it fell and lowered it to the ground, and then looked at the agent with a scared face to see how much he knew. The agent had leaped still farther away, and now was crouching, livid with fear, before this man whose last words had been words of delirium. No, he knew nothing. Pilchard alone knew the extent of his own deceit, which dead lips could never disclose. He alone knew of that half-formed idea he had not dared to mature, which had come to him a year ago when he looked at Swan's resolute face in the engine-room; and he alone in all the world could ever know of the terror which had possessed him at daybreak in the shanty when he had turned in a panic and run away—from what? ...

A MATTER OF RIVALRY

BY OCTAVE THANET

It was the fifth afternoon of St. Kunagunda's fair. An interlude of semi-rest had come between the clearing up last night's debris of crowd and traffic, which had filled the morning, and the renewed crowd and traffic that would come with the lamps. The tired elderly women in charge of the supper had sunk into chairs before their clean linen and dazzling white stone-china dishes and fresh bunches of lilacs. The pretty young girls at the "fancy table" were laughing and prattling rather loudly with two amiable young men who had been tacking home-made lace handkerchiefs and embroidered "art centres" in the vacant spaces left on the pink cambric wall by the departure of last night's purchases. A comely matron kept guard simultaneously over the useful but not perilously alluring wares of the "household table" and the adjacent temptations of the flower-stand and the candy-booth. The last was indeed fair to see, having a magnificent pyramid of pop-corn balls and entrancing heaps of bright-colored home-made French candy; and round and round its delights prowled a chubby and wistful boy, with hands in his penniless pockets, waiting for the chancellor of the exchequer.

Across the hall, the walls whereof were lavishly decked with red, white, and blue festoons of cambric, and had the green and gold of Erin's flag intertwined with the yellow and black of Germany, stood a table which had been the centre of interest for four nights, but which now was entirely deserted. There was no glory of color or pomp of bedizenment about it; nothing more taking to the eye than a ballot-box and a small show-case (the contents of the latter draped in newspapers at the present) and a neatly lettered sign above a blackboard, to one side. The sign simply demanded, "Vote Here!" The blackboard in less trim script announced that "For most popular business man" Mr. Timothy G. Finnerty had 305 votes, and three or four other candidates so few that there was no interest in deciphering the chalk figures; and that "For most popular young lady" Miss Norah Murray had 842 votes, and Miss Freda Berglund had 603. At intervals some one of the score of people in the hall would saunter up to the show-case or to the blackboard, to peer into the one or to study the figures on the other—although, really, there was no one in the hall who did not know every line on the board, and who had not seen both the gold watch and the gold-headed cane of the show-case. Two women came from different quarters of the room at the same instant to look at the blackboard. One was a comely dame in a silken gown that rustled and glittered with jet. She had just entered the hall, and was a little flushed with the climb up the stairs. The other was a stunted, wiry little Irish woman in black weeds of ancient make. She caught sight of the one in silk attire and paused. The first-comer also paused. Her color deepened; her head erected itself more proudly on her shoulders. Then she continued her progress, halting, with a dignified and elegant air, before the blackboard. The little Irish woman tossed her own head and appeared about to follow; however, her intention changed at a few words from the guardian of the apron table. She inclined her head, and with a glance of scorn at the silken back passed on over to the aprons and quilts.

The matrons at the supper-table had viewed the incident with interest. A little sigh of relief or regret rippled about the board.

"'Tis a great pity, that's sure," said one.

"I was there when they had the words," said another. "Mrs. Conner was saying this voting business was all wrong—"

"Well, sure she ain't far out of the way, with this time," interjected a voice; "bad blood more'n in this instance it's raised; the whole town's taking sides on it, and there was two fights yesterday. Why didn't they jest raffle the watch off decent and peaceable?"

"There's some objects to raffling."

"There's some objects to drinking tea an' coffee, they're so bigoted! In a raffle there's nobody pays more'n their quarter, or maybe a dollar or two—"

"And that's it. Look at the power o' money we're gettin', Mrs. O'Brien dear! We'd *niver* 'a' got nigh on to four hundred dollars for a gold watch rafflin'; and well you know it!"

"Maybe," agreed Mrs. O'Brien, grimly, "but neither would we have got fightin' out of the church and fightin' in it; nor Pat Barnes be having his head broke. 'Twas hurted awful bad he was. His own mother told me; and she said Fritz Miller was sick in bed from it; Pat paid him well for talkin' down ould Ireland; and poor Terry Flanagin, he lost his job at the saw-mill for maddin' the boss that's Dutch, and infidel Dutch at that; and there's quarrels on ivery side, God forgive 'em! They talk of it at the stores, and they talk of it at the saloon, where they do be going too often to talk it; and 'tis a shame an' a disgrace, down to that saloon the dirty Dutchman—"

"*Whisht!*" three or four mouths puckered in warning, and Mrs. O'Brien caught the smouldering gaze of a flaxen-haired woman in very full black skirts and black basque of an antique cut, who had but now approached the group; with her race's nimbleness of wit she added, "Sure there's dirty Germans and there's dirty Irish."

"Dere is," agreed the new-comer, with displeasing alacrity, "und some is in *dis* parish und dis sodality. I vas seen dem viping dishes mit a newsbaber. Dot's so. Yesterday night."

An electric thrill ran through the circle, and two matrons, suddenly very red, answered at once:

"Would you have us wipe them on our *handkerchiefs*? The towels were all gone!"

"'Twas the awful crowd did it; an' 'twas only some saucers for the ice-cream."

Mrs. O'Brien waved her hands, very clean, not very shapely, and worn by many an honest day's toil, persuading and pleading for peace at once. "Sure," says she, "if you'd wurrk at fairs you'd know that you can't be doing things like you'd do them at home; and 'twas only for a minit they wiped the saucers with the paper napkins, clean tishy-paper napkins, Mrs. Orendorf; 'twas only two or three saucers got wiped with the newspaper, because the napkins was give out and they was shrieking and clamoring for saucers; and they're *terrible*, them young girls! waving their hands and jumpin' an' squealin'. 'Me first, Mrs. O'Brien!' 'It's *my* turn, Mrs. O'Brien!' 'Oh, Mrs. O'Brien, wait on *me*. I've got six people haven't had a bite in half an hour; and they're so cross!' Till your mind's goin'! No doubt we're makin' money, but I'm for a smaller crowd an' more good falein'."

"It's for der voting dey kooms," grumbled the German woman, only half pacified. "Dot vas bad mistake haf dot votin'. Vot vas dot dirty Deutchman you call him do dot make you so mad?"

"Oh, it wasn't so *much*"—Mrs. O'Brien was still bent on peace—"he jist telephoned to the next door an' got the returns, as he called them, and had 'em posted up in his saloon. An' if they was daughters of mine—I 'ain't got anny daughters, praise God! for since I seen the way these waiters go on, I'm misdoubtin' I niver could manage thim—but if they was daughters of mine, 'twould be the sorry day for me whin they'd their names posted up in a saloon!"

"Meine fader in der old country kept a saloon," said the German woman, with extreme dryness of accent, "und does you mean to say vun vurd against Freda Berglund?"

"No, indade," cried Mrs. O'Brien.

"And do *you* mean to say one word against Norah Murray?" a bolder partisan on the Celtic side struck in, with a determined air. Three or four voices murmured assent.

The German stood her ground. "I nefer seen her till yesterday"—thus without committing direct assault on the Murray supporters she avoided concession; "all I know of her is dot she nefer haf dot gold vatch!"

"Then you know more than *we* do. Norah's ahead, and she'll be *more* ahead this evening," retorted a Murray voter; "there's plenty more money to spend for old Ireland—ain't there, ladies?"

"Whisht!" called the peace-maker, in her turn. "Ain't it easy to see how Mrs. Conner and Mrs. Finn come to words and hard falein' when we're nigh that same ourselves, we that determined to kape out of the worry? They are both awful nice, pretty young ladies, and I'm sorry such a question come up between them; and 'tis *dreadful*, O'Brien says, the way the young men was spinding their money for Norah last night. Sure, an' it is that. 'Tis all a bad thing; I think that like Mrs. Conner."

Mrs. Orendorf was unable to adjust her mental view to the varying argument; she cast a sullen and puzzled eye on the amiable Irish woman, and said, grimly:

"It isn't joost yoong mans vot kan spend money. Freda don't have got no yoong mans, 'cause her Schatz vent to der var und die py der fever in Florida—"

"Sure he did that!" cried Mrs. O'Brien, "an' 'twas a fine man an' a fine carpenter he was. Aw, the poor girl! I mind how she looked the day Company E marched out of town, him turnin' his eyes up sidewises, an' her white as paper but a-smilin'!"

"God pity her!" chimed in another matron, with the ready response to sympathy of the Celt. There was a little murmur of assent. Mrs. Orendorf's swelling crest fell a little; her tone was softer.

"But Freda got a fader, a goot man, *too* goot and kind; he say he vunt haf his dochter look down on like she don't got no friends. He go and mortgage his farm, und he got drie—tree hunterd dollar"—she tapped the sum off her palm with solemn deliberation—"und he svear he vill in der votin' all, all spend, an' sie git dot vatch. *Ach Himmel! er ist verruckt!* He say he got his pension and he got der insure on his life, und he 'ain't got nobody 'cept Freda, und he vunt haf Freda look down on. Und *sie* don't know. Mans don't can talk mit him; he git mad. He git mad at *me* 'cause I talk. *Dot's* vat der fine votin' do!"

A little gasp from the audience meant more than agreement; their eyes ran to Mrs. O'Brien, who faced the German and could see what they saw; then back of Mrs. Orendorf to the crimson face of a young girl. Mutely they signalled consternation.

But the young girl did not speak; she walked away quickly, not turning her head as she passed the voting-booth. She was a pretty girl, with fresh skin, the whiter and fresher against her abundant silky black hair and black-lashed violet eyes. She carried her dainty head a little haughtily, but her soft eyes had a wistful sweetness. Her big flowered hat and her white gown, brightened by blue ribbons, were as fresh as her skin and became her rich beauty. She walked with the natural light grace often seen in girls of her race, whatever their class. No one could watch the winsome little figure pass and not feel the charm of youth and frank innocence and immeasurable hopes. More than one pair of elderly eyes that had seen the glory and freshness of the dream fade followed it kindly and with a pensive pride.

"Ain't she pretty and slim!" sighed a stout lady in silk (Mrs. Conner, the most important supporter of the parish, no less), "and think of me having a waist as little as hers when I was married! But I wish she hadn't let them drag her into this voting business, for it has caused trouble."

"Norah's as good and sweet's she's pretty," another elderly woman replied. "Just to think of that young thing supporting her mother and educating her brother for a priest with only those pretty little hands! But she won't be doing it long if the boys can one of them get their way. And what will we do for a dress-maker then? We never *did* have such a stylish one!"

"That's so," Mrs. Conner agreed, cordially; "she's the only one I ever went to didn't make me look fleshier than I am. But I say it is all the more shame to make that innocent young creature talked about and fought over, and have jokes made in the saloon and at the stores, and quarrels outside the parish and in it, too."

"I guess it has gone farther than we thought," said the other. "Look! there's Father Kelly and the Vicar-General; they're looking at the blackboard. I wish I could hear what they are saying."

Norah, indeed, was the only person who did not look at the two quiet gentlemen before the blackboard, curiously, and wonder the same, since the voting-booth had become a firebrand menacing the peace of the parish. Norah was too busy with her own thoughts even to see them; she only wanted to get past her wellwishers and be alone with her perplexities. If she did not see her spiritual guides, they saw her, and Father Kelly's tired face brightened. "You really can't blame the boys," he said, smiling; "and she's as good a daughter and sister, and as good a girl, too, as ever stepped."

The Vicar-General smiled faintly, but his eyes were absent. The parish at Clover Hill was the newest in the diocese—a feeble folk struggling to build a church, or rather help build it, and holding its first bazar. There were no rich people of their faith—unless one except the Conners, who owned the saw-mill and were well-to-do—not even many poor to club their mites; more disheartening yet, the parish roll held about an equal proportion of Irish and German names. The Vicar-General and the Bishop shook their heads at the yoking of the two races; but there was no church nearer than Father Kelly's, five miles away, and Father Kelly was not young, and his own great parish growing all the time; so the parish was made, and a young American priest, who had more sense than always goes with burning enthusiasm, was sent to guide the souls at Clover Hill and keep the peace. He kept it until the fair, when in an evil hour he consented to the voting-booth. He expected—they all expected—that the excitement would focus on the gold-headed cane, and that Mr. Michael Conner would lead the poll, although the popular Finnerty might give him a pretty race for his honors; the gold watch was but an incidental attraction to please the young people and attract outsiders; nor was there any suggestion of names. Alas! Michael Conner, a blunt man, dubbed the voting scheme a "d—weather-breeder," and would not give the use of his name; hence there was a walkaway for Finnerty; and somehow, before any of the elders quite realized how it began, the Irish girl and the German girl were unconsciously setting the whole town by the ears, and imported voters from Father Kelly's were joyously mixing in the fight.

"There's no question about the *need* of stopping it," said the Vicar-General, continuing his own train of thought aloud, "but how are we to do it? The feeling is a perfect dynamite factory now, and the least stumble on our part will bring an explosion. If we tried to give them the money back—and you know women have a tight grip on money—we shouldn't know where to give it. Positively we're like the family of the poor fellow who had the fit—one doctor said it would kill him to bring him to his senses, and the other said he would die if they didn't!"

"And Father Martin safe in his bed with pneumonia!" groaned Father Kelly.

Norah had found her progress barred by new-comers, and she had fled back to avoid them. Her cheeks reddened again, and the tears burned her eyelids; she went past too fast for more than a hurried salutation, at which Father Kelly shook his head. "That's the girl, isn't it?" said the Vicar-General. "I'm afraid the situation is a little too much for her, too; she looks excited."

"Not a bit, not a bit," cried Father Kelly, undaunted; "she's a bit impulsive, but she's got good sense."

"She wears too much jewelry."

Norah did not hear this; she was out of the hall, speeding back to Mrs. Conner's gown that awaited her finishing touches. Her mother, a little creature with sweet temper that made amends for an entire lack of energy, was rocking over some bastings, sawing the air with her forefinger as she discoursed on the weighty splendor of the gold watch and chain, ending in gush of parental complacency, "And Norah says it'll be as much mine 's hers!"

Norah could hear her chirping on, happily, while she laid away her hat in the bandbox and girt herself with a protecting apron.

The talk turned her cold. "It ain't only for myself I want it," she declared to an invisible suggester, "though I *do* want something real. I never had a real gold chain, or even a real gold breastpin, in my life—or a ring. Oh, I did want one!" She looked scornfully at the gay prism gleaming from her pretty fingers (fingers as daintily kept as any lady's); they had flashed like rubies and sapphires and diamonds from the white velvet drifts of the show-case in the great department store where she bought them when she went to the city; but now they were cheapened and dimmed by her memories of the "real" watch. She peeled them roughly from her hands.

She had no morsel of news ready for the hungry ears awaiting her. To her mother's questions she answered briefly that the only thing she heard was that Freda Berglund would have a great number of new votes in the evening.

Mrs. Murray tossed back a confident: *"Let* her! I know some boys that's going to go this night, with a hundred dollars in their pockets each of 'em. Let her bring on her votes, I say. It's a good cause gits the money. But it's you'll be wearin' the watch next Sunday, and not Freda Berglund!"

Norah bit her lip. She was not used to silence, but she sewed silently (Norah, who was so sweet-tempered that she had been known to work a whole day with a machine that skipped stitches, never getting cross, and stopping four times to wrestle with the bobbin before she subdued it). Her mother did not know what to make of her. Her own nickering complaints of Norah's "glumness" sank into dumb anxiety. She stole timid glances at the bowed black head and the frowning black brows; after a glance she would sigh, a prolonged, patient sigh. There are times when a sigh is to strained nerves like a blast of hot air on a burn. Norah jumped up and ran away from her own irritation before it exploded. She made a pretext of looking at her skirt (which was new) in the parlor cheval-glass; but in the parlor, behind the door, she did not give a glance to the picture in the mirror. The "pire glass," as Mrs. Murray called it, was a relic of the family's better days when Norah's father was alive and kept a grocery-store and owned a horse and wagon; its florid frame of black-walnut etched with gilt, its tall mirror, very little marred by water-spots on the back, long had been reverently admired by Norah; it showed that the family had "had things"; but she passed it without a glance, just as she passed the cabinet organ decked in flowered plush which she had bought with her own savings. Never until that day had she stood in the parlor without a sensation of pleasure over its fresh paint and paper and the many gilt frames on the wall; but to-day she went, unnoting, to the crayon picture of a man, and looked through tears at a plain, smiling, kindly face.

"I wish you hadn't died," was all she said; but the tears rolled down her cheeks and her frame shook with sobs that she forced to be noiseless. At last she dried her wet cheeks and tossed her head. "I don't see that *I* need do *anything*," she muttered, while she hurried round the house outside, in order that she might reach the bedroom and efface the traces of her weeping. "I'm a great fool to think of doing anything," she declared. "I didn't put myself up, and I won't put myself down—and disappoint mother and all my friends. It's none of my business." Therewith she assumed a light and cheerful air, which she carried securely through the remainder of the afternoon.

* * * * *

The fifth evening of St. Kunagunda's fair opened with a stifling crowd. Protestants, Catholics, and Germans who never had seen the interior of an American church jostled the buyers at the booths, and the faithful dutifully ate turkey and cold rolls for the fifth time at the supper-tables. The outsiders did not linger at the booths; they were come to vote or to witness the voting, and their jests and comments buzzed noisily above the talk. Every moment the note of the buzz grew more hostile. More than a few ears were tingling; at every turn there were scowls and sullen eyes and ugly smiles. The matrons' cheeks were burning; their eyes flashed; every now and again one of their voices shrilled defiantly above the hoarse hum of the crowd. The young Irish girls were laughing, enjoying the excitement, and admiring the young men flaunting their banknotes with the swing of their father's shillalahs. The young German girls curled their lips and whispered together. There was a significant herding of the contending races apart, while the visiting Anglo-Saxons wore an air of safe and dispassionate enjoyment, such as pertains of right to the boy on the fence waiting for the fight.

Norah Murray had a circle of young men about her, who laughed rapturously at her sallies. She wore her chain and a new rhinestone brooch and all her rings. She looked very handsome with her flushed cheeks and bright eyes. She raised her voice to be heard above the din. Mrs. Murray's new bonnet nodded its red roses and black ostrich tips among the lace handkerchiefs and embroidery of the fancy table—she being enthroned on the step-ladder for lack of other seat—and her delighted eyes ran from her daughter to the voting blackboard. She waved a spangled fan and smiled buoyantly at every familiar face, whether turned towards her in recognition or not. Mrs. O'Brien, who had slipped away from the kitchen to be sure the lamps were not smoking, stopped a moment beside her. Mrs. O'Brien looked tired and worried when she let her own smile of greeting slip from her face. A tinge of the same expression was on Father Kelly's kind old countenance, but the Vicar-General's features were as inscrutable as a doctor's. He had made a genial procession through the room, distributing the merited praise at each booth, and appreciably softening the atmosphere by his presence. He halted opposite Norah's party. Father Kelly's gaze grew anxious. "I mind me," said he—"I mind me of the child when her father died—not six she was—holding her mother's hand, not weeping herself, the creature, just stroking her mother's hand and petting her; and holding the baby, the one that's off to the seminary now. Her father was an honest man. He failed once, and then paid every dollar with interest—an *honest* man. I mind me of little Norah at her first communion—"

The Vicar-General smiled. "Kelly, you're a good fellow," said he, not removing his glance from Norah's excited face.

"She'll come out all right, all right," said Father Kelly, with the hammer-like gesture of his right fist which his congregation knew well for a storm signal. "She's a good girl. This is no fault of hers, this foolish contraption to make money; I'm one with Conner, there; but the girls aren't to blame. Freda's a good girl, too. That's she coming."

The German heroine of this miniature Nibelungenlied was tall and slender, fair haired and fair faced. Her face wore a placid air; she looked perfectly serene and had assumed unconsciousness as a garment; she did not talk, only faintly smiled in return to the greetings that met her on every side. To right and left, before and behind her, walked her two aunts and her two neighbors, women of substance and dignity. They walled her about as might a body-guard, sending eye-blinks of defiance at the hilarious young Irishmen. Mrs. Orendorf, of the guard, went the length of twisting her head for a final glare of disapproval at Norah, in passing. Norah laughed. "I used to know Freda Burglund last week," said she, "but I guess she has forgotten me."

"She's too busy with the blackboard, doing arithmetic," joked one of the young men.

"You ought to see old Fritz!" cried another; "he's clean off his base. He's mortgaged his farm to Nichols. Nichols didn't want to lend, but he would have the money."

"Well, I guess we'll give him a run for his pile."

"He's mortgaged his farm!" said a third young man; when his voiced sounded, the very slightest of movements of Norah's head betrayed that she listened.

"I'd mortgage two farms if I had them," was the gallant comment from the first man, "if Miss Norah needed votes."

The third man felt the rustle of every dollar he had, drawn out of the bank that morning, and now bulging his waistcoat-pocket in company with a bit of ribbon that had dropped from Norah's hair; but it was easier for him to make money than talk; he was ready to push the last of it over the voting-table for Norah, but he wasn't ready of tongue; he put his big honest hands in his pocket, and lest he should glower too openly at the fluent blade, sent his eyes after Freda Berglund's yellow head and fine shoulders. Norah could see him. She stiffened.

"I don't think it very nice of her to *let* her father mortgage his farm," said a fourth partisan of Norah's; "he'd better buy her a watch out and out; you can get a good one for ten dollars. She'd ought to stop the old man. Her mother would if she were alive."

"Fritz ain't so easy headed off," said the third man. "Miss Freda is a very nice young lady; I don't believe she knows about it."

He kept his eyes on the yellow head, this unfortunate bungler, who had been in love with Norah since he had worn knickerbockers, and Norah held her own head higher in the air. And she let Mr. Williamson, the new book-keeper at Conner's (he who would have mortgaged two farms for her), take her to the ice-cream table, leaving the bungling lover (christened Patrick Maurice, his surname being Barnes), to jostle dismally over to the apron table, where Freda was.

Norah laughed at Mr. Williamson's jokes, and asked him questions about the business college from which he had recently been graduated, and was the picture of soft animation and pleasure; and the while her heart was like lead, and she hated Freda Berglund. Sitting at the table she heard snatches of talk, all tinctured by the strong excitement of the evening. "I can't help it if they do quarrel," she thought, angrily, answering her own accusation; not even to herself did she say that she hated Freda.

Her eyes wandered a second over the hall; they saw the Vicar-General's pale, handsome face, a half-head taller than Father Kelly's good gray head; they saw a square-jawed, black-haired, determined, smiling young man behind the ballot-box turning his eyes from Pat Barnes to an elderly man who held up his hand, waving a roll of bills.

"Ah, I see Berglund has arrived," said Williamson. "You are going to do a lot to build the church, Miss Norah."

Berglund was rather a short man; his hair was gray; he limped from the old wound received at Shiloh. Something clutched at Norah's heart as she looked at him. Williamson made some trivial joke; she did not hear it; she was hearing over again the words of the German woman to Mrs. O'Brien that afternoon. Impulsively she sprang to her feet. "Will you excuse me, Mr. Williamson?" she exclaimed. "I have to go to the voting-booth one moment." She went so swiftly that Williamson had much ado to keep pace with her, besides overpaying the waitress in his hurry. Father Kelly swallowed a groan of dismay at the fresh strain on his faith when he perceived her beckoning a ring-laden hand at the custodian of votes; and the Vicar-General involuntarily frowned. They both with one accord pushed up to the table—to the visible relief of the young man behind it. "I don't know what to do," he confided to Father Kelly, before the latter could ask the question quivering on his tongue—"I don't know what to do. Miss Murray wants me not to take in any more money 'til I hear from her again. She'll be back. And here's old Berglund wants three hundred and fifty dollars' worth for Miss Freda, and here's Barnes with a big bunch for Miss Murray, trying to scare off the old man. What'll I do, Father?"

"I guess you better not do anything," said Father Kelly, with a twinkle in his eye. "Norah Murray is apt to have a good reason for her asking. Shut the booth down, and *I'll* take charge while you go off for a cup of coffee."

The Vicar-General nodded approval.

"Well, just's you say, Father," said the young man; "it's kind of unprecedented."

"What do you suppose it means?" puzzled the Vicar-General, in an undertone, as the vote-taker disappeared; and the crowd fell back a little on Father Kelly's bland announcement that Mr. Duffy had been called off for a few minutes, and there would be a recess in voting.

"'Tis beyond *me*," said Father Kelly, "but watch the girl; she's gone straight to Freda Berglund. There, they're talking; they're going off together with Mrs. Orendorf. I can't give a guess, but she's a good girl. I'm hopeful."

Norah had indeed gone straight to Freda Berglund. She addressed her in so low a voice that only Freda and Mrs. Orendorf, bending across Freda's shoulders at that instant, the better to cheapen a darning-bag for stockings, could hear her words. "I want to see you, Freda," she said. "Won't you and Mrs. Orendorf come away somewhere so we can talk? I have got something important to say."

"I—don't—know," faltered Freda.

"I want Mrs. O'Brien, too," said Norah, firmly. "It's all right; you'll think it all right, Mrs. Orendorf. Come, come; don't you see those men who have been drinking? Don't you hear them? Don't you see Mrs. Finn, who used to think there was nobody like Mrs. Conner, looking the other way so's not to see her? Can't you hear the quarrelling all round? They've stopped voting, but they haven't stopped quarrelling. Come!"

Although she had dropped her voice, the listeners were so close that they caught snatches of the sentences, and craned their necks forward and hushed their own talk to listen. Mrs. Orendorf was not of a nimble habit of thought; but she felt the electric impetus of the Irish girl; besides, was *she* not bidden? Could she not protect Freda from the machinations of the enemy?

"Dot's so, Freda," she concluded, stolidly. "Koom den, der only blace vere we can talk py uns is dot coal-closet wo is der eggstry ice-cream freezer. Koom. I see Meezis O'Breen."

Amid a startling pause, every eye questioning them, the three picked up Mrs. O'Brien and sought the coal-closet. Then Norah turned. In the dim light her face shone whitely. Her full melodious voice shook the least in the world with haste and excitement. "We've got to stop this," said she, "and I know how. Freda, I am going to withdraw my name. I wish to Heaven I never had let them put it on. You may have the watch."

Freda's tall figure was only an outline in the shadow; they could not see her face; but the outline wavered backward. Her voice was stiff and cold.

"I don't think that's fair. You have more votes than I have."

Mrs. O'Brien opened her lips and shut them tightly. It was so dark no one saw her, or Mrs. Orendorf, as she sat on the freezer gulping down inaudible opinions regarding Norah's sanity.

"I sha'n't have," retorted Norah, impatiently, "when your

father spends all his money that he mortgaged his farm—"

"What!" cried Freda.

"She not know; ve keep it von her," muttered Mrs. Orendorf. "Fritz make me promise not to tell."

"Well, he didn't make *me*," said Norah. "*I'll* tell. He raised the money, and he was trying to buy the votes, and I saw him. I haven't any father. I can't remember anything of my father except his leading me about when I was a little thing by the finger, and how kind his voice was; but I miss him—I miss him all the time; I know he was a good man, and loved me; and he'd have done anything for me, just as your father is doing; and I couldn't have borne it to have him, and I was sure you couldn't, either. Freda, it's all wrong, this spending more money than they can afford on us; I've felt it all along. Now let's stop it. The church has got enough."

"Is it true about papa?" said Freda, in German.

"*Ach Himmel*! Yes, my child. Dost thou not know thy father yet? For all he seems still and stern, thou art more than all the world to him." Mrs. Orendorf spoke in the same tongue; her other listeners could not understand it, but they marvelled over the soft change in her voice.

"It's true enough, Miss Freda," said Mrs. O'Brien, gently. "And maybe you're in the right of it, Norah darling, though 'tis a bit hard to give in; but, yes, I'm sure you're right."

"You *are* right," said Freda, "and it's all been wrong, all wrong. But I've got to see my father first. Please come with me."

As Norah had led them in the first place, Freda led them by an equally potent although entirely different force now; it was Norah's turn to follow, blindly.

A hush everywhere in their wake betrayed that a conscious-ness of their conference and its importance was in the air. Freda was pale, Norah's cheeks burned, but neither girl looked to the right or the left; and both the matrons following avoided their friends' curiosity by a soldierly "eyes front." Freda walked up to her father, who looked up, not altogether pleased, at her light touch on his arm.

"This is no place for thee, my child," said he; something in her face made his voice gentler than common. She looked, he thought, dimly, as she had looked when they got the news about Otto.

"I *have* to say something," said Freda.

"You beples stand back!" commanded Mrs. Orendorf, with a backward impulse of her elbows.

"Yes, you stand back, ladies and gentlemen, please," begged Mrs. O'Brien, smiling; "'twill all be explained to yous." Only Norah stood her ground; and Pat Barnes kept in the front rank of the bystanders.

"What is it?" growled Berglund, bristling at the circle of faces much readier for peace than war.

"She wants to give the watch to me," explained Freda, rapidly repeating almost word for word Norah's offer. As she spoke suspicion wrinkled the corners of old Fritz's eyes.

"Maypi sie know sie vill git peten," he muttered, loud enough for Norah to hear. Then, as he saw her color turn, his hard face softened. "No," he said, clearly, "it don't be *dot*; dot Pat Barnes got his pocket full of moneys; no, sie is a goot schild, und her fader he vas a goot mans; sie haf a hard dime mit no fader to look oudt for her." He turned to Norah, whose swimming eyes met his full. Pat Barnes tried to cough down his emotion and made a strange squeak; but nobody smiled; the crowded hall was curiously still as Fritz limped up to Norah. "No, ve don't can take it off you; can ve, Freda?" said he.

Freda slipped her hand into her father's arm. "No, Norah," she said. "I withdraw my name. And I'm prouder to have my father than all the watches in the world!"

"Sure, you're right there, mavourneen," cried Mrs. O'Brien. "Whisht, all of you! These blessid children have got the way out of all this mess; they're better Christians than anny of us." Mrs. Orendorf frowned fiercely, reached for her handkerchief, and wiped her face.

Father Kelly felt it time for his own word, and stepped into the circle. A sentence or two from Mrs. O'Brien made the quick-witted old Irishman master of the incident.

"As I understand it," his full, rich, Celtic tones purred, "'tis the feeling of both these young ladies that there is hard feeling and strife and wasteful spending of money coming out of what was meant to be a good-natured contest for the good of the church; but this disputing, this spending, are neither for the good of the church nor the glory of God—far from it—God forgive us our weakness. So both these young ladies withdrew their names. We have cause to be proud of them both, as they surely have cause to be proud of the loyalty of their friends." (Irrepressible applause.) "And the kindest thing their friends can do is to shake hands all around." (A voice—in point of fact, the voice of the widow Murray: "But what will the sodality do with the watch?") "The watch is the property of the parish." Here Father Kelly paused, his persuasive argument rolling back on himself; *he didn't* know what to do with the watch. It was too perilous to run the risk of new discords over it. The priest cast a distress rocket in a look at the Vicar-General; but the Vicar-General perfidiously smiled and looked away.

Up spoke Norah, her sweet voice not quite steady, her cheeks crimson—but they all heard her: "It's a large gold watch. Why can't we give it to Father Kelly?"

The Vicar-General's lifted hand stilled the shout that rose.

"Why not?" called he. "Father Kelly is not a young lady, but he is popular."

And Father Kelly, putting both hands over his blushes, ran away from the frantic roar of applause and laughter. The Vicar-General pursued him to say:

"You were right, Kelly; she *is* a good girl—and a wise one!"

Perhaps the only person in the hall who was not either shouting or screaming, according to sex, was Norah's mother; and the cloud on her face lightened when she saw Norah coming to her on Pat Barnes's arm and Pat's face aglow.

Freda saw them too; she slipped her hand into her father's arm.

"*Liebchen*!" said he, stroking it with his rough fingers, "I will get thee a watch some day, never fear!"

But it was not the thought of a watch that made Freda's heart lighter than for many a day. "I don't want a watch," said she. "Oh, I'm sorry for Norah, who can't even remember about her father!"

Choose from Thousands of 1stWorldLibrary Classics By

A. M. Barnard	Booth Tarkington	Edward Everett Hale
Ada Leverson	Boyd Cable	Edward J. O'Biren
Adolphus William Ward	Bram Stoker	Edward S. Ellis
Aesop	C. Collodi	Edwin L. Arnold
Agatha Christie	C. E. Orr	Eleanor Atkins
Alexander Aaronsohn	C. M. Ingleby	Eleanor Hallowell Abbott
Alexander Kielland	Carolyn Wells	Eliot Gregory
Alexandre Dumas	Catherine Parr Traill	Elizabeth Gaskell
Alfred Gatty	Charles A. Eastman	Elizabeth McCracken
Alfred Ollivant	Charles Amory Beach	Elizabeth Von Arnim
Alice Duer Miller	Charles Dickens	Ellem Key
Alice Turner Curtis	Charles Dudley Warner	Emerson Hough
Alice Dunbar	Charles Farrar Browne	Emilie F. Carlen
Allen Chapman	Charles Ives	Emily Bronte
Alleyne Ireland	Charles Kingsley	Emily Dickinson
Ambrose Bierce	Charles Klein	Enid Bagnold
Amelia E. Barr	Charles Hanson Towne	Enilor Macartney Lane
Amory H. Bradford	Charles Lathrop Pack	Erasmus W. Jones
Andrew Lang	Charles Romyn Dake	Ernie Howard Pie
Andrew McFarland Davis	Charles Whibley	Ethel May Dell
Andy Adams	Charles Willing Beale	Ethel Turner
Angela Brazil	Charlotte M. Braeme	Ethel Watts Mumford
Anna Alice Chapin	Charlotte M. Yonge	Eugene Sue
Anna Sewell	Charlotte Perkins Stetson	Eugenie Foa
Annie Besant	Clair W. Hayes	Eugene Wood
Annie Hamilton Donnell	Clarence Day Jr.	Eustace Hale Ball
Annie Payson Call	Clarence E. Mulford	Evelyn Everett-green
Annie Roe Carr	Clemence Housman	Everard Cotes
Annonaymous	Confucius	F. H. Cheley
Anton Chekhov	Coningsby Dawson	F. J. Cross
Archibald Lee Fletcher	Cornelis DeWitt Wilcox	F. Marion Crawford
Arnold Bennett	Cyril Burleigh	Fannie E. Newberry
Arthur C. Benson	D. H. Lawrence	Federick Austin Ogg
Arthur Conan Doyle	Daniel Defoe	Ferdinand Ossendowski
Arthur M. Winfield	David Garnett	Fergus Hume
Arthur Ransome	Dinah Craik	Florence A. Kilpatrick
Arthur Schnitzler	Don Carlos Janes	Fremont B. Deering
Arthur Train	Donald Keyhoe	Francis Bacon
Atticus	Dorothy Kilner	Francis Darwin
B.H. Baden-Powell	Dougan Clark	Frances Hodgson Burnett
B. M. Bower	Douglas Fairbanks	Frances Parkinson Keyes
B. C. Chatterjee	E. Nesbit	Frank Gee Patchin
Baroness Emmuska Orczy	E. P. Roe	Frank Harris
Baroness Orczy	E. Phillips Oppenheim	Frank Jewett Mather
Basil King	E. S. Brooks	Frank L. Packard
Bayard Taylor	Earl Barnes	Frank V. Webster
Ben Macomber	Edgar Rice Burroughs	Frederic Stewart Isham
Bertha Muzzy Bower	Edith Van Dyne	Frederick Trevor Hill
Bjornstjerne Bjornson	Edith Wharton	Frederick Winslow Taylor

Friedrich Kerst	Hayden Carruth	James Branch Cabell
Friedrich Nietzsche	Helent Hunt Jackson	James DeMille
Fyodor Dostoyevsky	Helen Nicolay	James Joyce
G.A. Henty	Hendrik Conscience	James Lane Allen
G.K. Chesterton	Hendy David Thoreau	James Lane Allen
Gabrielle E. Jackson	Henri Barbusse	James Oliver Curwood
Garrett P. Serviss	Henrik Ibsen	James Oppenheim
Gaston Leroux	Henry Adams	James Otis
George A. Warren	Henry Ford	James R. Driscoll
George Ade	Henry Frost	Jane Abbott
Geroge Bernard Shaw	Henry James	Jane Austen
George Cary Eggleston	Henry Jones Ford	Jane L. Stewart
George Durston	Henry Seton Merriman	Janet Aldridge
George Ebers	Henry W Longfellow	Jens Peter Jacobsen
George Eliot	Herbert A. Giles	Jerome K. Jerome
George Gissing	Herbert Carter	Jessie Graham Flower
George MacDonald	Herbert N. Casson	John Buchan
George Meredith	Herman Hesse	John Burroughs
George Orwell	Hildegard G. Frey	John Cournos
George Sylvester Viereck	Homer	John F. Kennedy
George Tucker	Honore De Balzac	John Gay
George W. Cable	Horace B. Day	John Glasworthy
George Wharton James	Horace Walpole	John Habberton
Gertrude Atherton	Horatio Alger Jr.	John Joy Bell
Gordon Casserly	Howard Pyle	John Kendrick Bangs
Grace E. King	Howard R. Garis	John Milton
Grace Gallatin	Hugh Lofting	John Philip Sousa
Grace Greenwood	Hugh Walpole	John Taintor Foote
Grant Allen	Humphry Ward	Jonas Lauritz Idemil Lie
Guillermo A. Sherwell	Ian Maclaren	Jonathan Swift
Gulielma Zollinger	Inez Haynes Gillmore	Joseph A. Altsheler
Gustav Flaubert	Irving Bacheller	Joseph Carey
H. A. Cody	Isabel Cecilia Williams	Joseph Conrad
H. B. Irving	Isabel Hornibrook	Joseph E. Badger Jr
H.C. Bailey	Israel Abrahams	Joseph Hergesheimer
H. G. Wells	Ivan Turgenev	Joseph Jacobs
H. H. Munro	J.G.Austin	Jules Vernes
H. Irving Hancock	J. Henri Fabre	Julian Hawthrone
H. R. Naylor	J. M. Barrie	Julie A Lippmann
H. Rider Haggard	J. M. Walsh	Justin Huntly McCarthy
H. W. C. Davis	J. Macdonald Oxley	Kakuzo Okakura
Haldeman Julius	J. R. Miller	Karle Wilson Baker
Hall Caine	J. S. Fletcher	Kate Chopin
Hamilton Wright Mabie	J. S. Knowles	Kenneth Grahame
Hans Christian Andersen	J. Storer Clouston	Kenneth McGaffey
Harold Avery	J. W. Duffield	Kate Langley Bosher
Harold McGrath	Jack London	Kate Langley Bosher
Harriet Beecher Stowe	Jacob Abbott	Katherine Cecil Thurston
Harry Castlemon	James Allen	Katherine Stokes
Harry Coghill	James Andrews	L. A. Abbot
Harry Houidini	James Baldwin	L. T. Meade

L. Frank Baum
Latta Griswold
Laura Dent Crane
Laura Lee Hope
Laurence Housman
Lawrence Beasley
Leo Tolstoy
Leonid Andreyev
Lewis Carroll
Lewis Sperry Chafer
Lilian Bell
Lloyd Osbourne
Louis Hughes
Louis Joseph Vance
Louis Tracy
Louisa May Alcott
Lucy Fitch Perkins
Lucy Maud Montgomery
Luther Benson
Lydia Miller Middleton
Lyndon Orr
M. Corvus
M. H. Adams
Margaret E. Sangster
Margret Howth
Margaret Vandercook
Margaret W. Hungerford
Margret Penrose
Maria Edgeworth
Maria Thompson Daviess
Mariano Azuela
Marion Polk Angellotti
Mark Overton
Mark Twain
Mary Austin
Mary Catherine Crowley
Mary Cole
Mary Hastings Bradley
Mary Roberts Rinehart
Mary Rowlandson
M. Wollstonecraft Shelley
Maud Lindsay
Max Beerbohm
Myra Kelly
Nathaniel Hawthrone
Nicolo Machiavelli
O. F. Walton
Oscar Wilde

Owen Johnson
P.G. Wodehouse
Paul and Mabel Thorne
Paul G. Tomlinson
Paul Severing
Percy Brebner
Percy Keese Fitzhugh
Peter B. Kyne
Plato
Quincy Allen
R. Derby Holmes
R. L. Stevenson
R. S. Ball
Rabindranath Tagore
Rahul Alvares
Ralph Bonehill
Ralph Henry Barbour
Ralph Victor
Ralph Waldo Emmerson
Rene Descartes
Ray Cummings
Rex Beach
Rex E. Beach
Richard Harding Davis
Richard Jefferies
Richard Le Gallienne
Robert Barr
Robert Frost
Robert Gordon Anderson
Robert L. Drake
Robert Lansing
Robert Lynd
Robert Michael Ballantyne
Robert W. Chambers
Rosa Nouchette Carey
Rudyard Kipling
Saint Augustine
Samuel B. Allison
Samuel Hopkins Adams
Sarah Bernhardt
Sarah C. Hallowell
Selma Lagerlof
Sherwood Anderson
Sigmund Freud
Standish O'Grady
Stanley Weyman
Stella Benson
Stella M. Francis

Stephen Crane
Stewart Edward White
Stijn Streuvels
Swami Abhedananda
Swami Parmananda
T. S. Ackland
T. S. Arthur
The Princess Der Ling
Thomas A. Janvier
Thomas A Kempis
Thomas Anderton
Thomas Bailey Aldrich
Thomas Bulfinch
Thomas De Quincey
Thomas Dixon
Thomas H. Huxley
Thomas Hardy
Thomas More
Thornton W. Burgess
U. S. Grant
Upton Sinclair
Valentine Williams
Various Authors
Vaughan Kester
Victor Appleton
Victor G. Durham
Victoria Cross
Virginia Woolf
Wadsworth Camp
Walter Camp
Walter Scott
Washington Irving
Wilbur Lawton
Wilkie Collins
Willa Cather
Willard F. Baker
William Dean Howells
William le Queux
W. Makepeace Thackeray
William W. Walter
William Shakespeare
Winston Churchill
Yei Theodora Ozaki
Yogi Ramacharaka
Young E. Allison
Zane Grey